VICTORIAN MEMORIAL BRASSES

VICTORIAN MEMORIAL BRASSES
David Meara

ROUTLEDGE & KEGAN PAUL
London, Boston, Melbourne and Henley

First published in 1983
by Routledge & Kegan Paul Ltd
39 Store Street, London WC1E 7DD,
Broadway House, Newtown Road,
Henley-on-Thames, Oxon RG9 1EN,
9 Park Street, Boston, Mass. 02108, USA and
296 Beaconsfield Parade,
Middle Park, Melbourne 3206, Australia

Set in Baskerville by
Rowland Phototypesetting, Bury St Edmunds, Suffolk
and printed in Great Britain by
BAS Printers, Stockbridge, Hampshire

© *David Meara 1983*

Library of Congress Cataloging in Publication Data
Meara, David, 1947–
Victorian memorial brasses.
1. Brasses, Victorian – Great Britain. I. Title.
NB1842.M37   1982   739'.522'0941   82-13162

ISBN 0-7100-9312-8 (pbk.)

TO MY MOTHER AND FATHER

Contents

Illustrations

Introduction

You may well have seen some of the medieval brasses which lie on the floors of our parish churches. What you are much less likely to have noticed are their successors – the Victorian and modern brasses, ranging from figures under resplendent canopies to simple inscription plates, which adorn church walls and floors in their thousands. For many years they have been unrecognised and neglected, but recently they have begun to receive serious attention. Undoubtedly many inscription plates of the period are insignificant, if not positively unattractive. But between the years 1840 and 1920 a very large number of figure brasses and elaborate inscriptions were produced, which are artistically distinguished, and well worth studying in their own right.

Many of those commemorated were distinguished members of society, or famous men and women of their day. Not only are a number of the great Victorian architects represented in brass, but also bishops, archbishops, soldiers, an American president, and members of the aristocracy. The origin of the revival in the Oxford Movement has always meant that brasses have been regarded as a 'high church' form of memorial, and by far the largest number were laid down to clergymen. But all sections of society have been represented over the years.

Two modern prejudices need to be set aside when studying Victorian brass design: first, that which favours plainness. The Victorians saw no virtue in this, and instead revelled in richness, ornament and colour. Second, that which rejects historicism, the conscious use of the past as a source of design inspiration for the present. Victorian designers felt that historical models lent an additional richness to their designs. If the observer understood the historical examples that were being copied or adapted, this would give added depth to his appreciation of the particular work of art. If the reader can set these prejudices aside I think he will find Victorian brasses to be attractive, original, and capable of standing alongside the best products of the art of the Gothic Revival.

Victorian and modern brasses are subject to the same kind of stresses and dangers as medieval brasses, but without the protection that extreme age affords. They are often on cathedral floors and walked over daily by tourists, as in Westminster Abbey. There the Keeper of the Muniments is very much aware of the problem, but elsewhere church authorities are often ignorant of their existence. Their care and conservation is vital and urgent, and it is hoped that this book will help to bring them to the attention of the public.

Acknowledgments

This book could not have been written without the help and encouragement of a great many people. The author is greatly indebted to the clergy who have supplied information and allowed rubbings to be made or photographs taken of the brasses in their care. The author is also very grateful to the staffs of numerous museums and libraries for the readiness with which they have offered their facilities, and wishes in particular to thank the staff of Reading University Library and Miss E. Leary of the Birmingham Museum and Art Gallery. It would not have been possible to include so many illustrations without the painstaking work and ready help of the staff of the Photographic Unit at Reading University, and to them the author offers his sincere thanks.

The author is also most grateful to Mr Richard Busby, Mr Patrick Farman, Mr Derek Chivers, Mr and Mrs H. Grimes, Mr Stan Budd and Mr Christopher Byrom for the generous loan of their rubbings, and to Mr Jack Bainbridge, Mr Peter Lambert, Mr Peter Heseltine and Mr Paul Cockerham for information and the loan of photographs. Similarly his sincere thanks go to Mrs M. Edwards for her unfailing help in the difficult task of preparing and typing the manuscript, to Mrs M. Button, Mrs S. Dewar and Miss J. Ware for their invaluable secretarial assistance, and to Mrs D. Fincham for her encouragement and advice on numerous technical problems. Lastly, and above all, to Rosemary, for her unfailing support and patience, the author offers his love and gratitude.

ACKNOWLEDGMENTS

The author and publishers would like to thank the following for permission to reproduce photographs included in this book: Victoria and Albert Museum: 28, 35, 43, 44, 48; National Museum of Wales: 8, 12, 14; Dean and Chapter, Westminster Abbey: 45; Birmingham Museum and Art Gallery: 16, 17, 18, 20; John Hardman Studios: 15; Monumental Brass Society: 1.

NOTES

All references to county locations in this book are in accordance with county boundaries as they were before the local government re-organisation of the 1970s.

All measurements are given in inches, height preceding width.

THE
REVIVAL
BEGINS

The genesis of the Gothic Revival can be seen in the novels of Sir Walter Scott, who popularised in the eighteenth century the romantic appeal of the Middle Ages. The first significant monument to this spirit of antiquarianism is usually considered to be Horace Walpole's villa, Strawberry Hill, the reconstruction of which began in 1750. It is of interest in the present context because the 'winding cloisters' of the house originally contained a fine memorial brass to Bishop Ralph Walpole of Ely (d. 1301) (plate 1) which Horace Walpole had commissioned from a Swiss painter, Johann Heinrich Muntz (1727 –98). Walpole presumably laid it down to add a touch of realism to his fairy-tale mansion – a medieval ancestor commemorated in the romantic cloister. But there was nothing spontaneous about Strawberry Hill; it was part of the 'Romantic Revival' and lacked the genius of later Gothic art and architecture. It was at best an amusing occupation for a gentleman at leisure, and a contrast to the prevailing fashion for things Grecian.

During this period antiquaries, such as Richard Gough, John Carter and John Britton (commemorated by a brass in Salisbury Cathedral), wrote about architecture, medieval art, and memorial brasses, and many began to take impressions of brasses by inking the plates and making prints off the surface. The most famous exponents of this practice were Craven Ord and John Cullum, who made a large collection of impressions off brasses in East Anglia and the Midlands, which are now in the British Museum. Another antiquary who wrote about brasses was John Sell Cotman (1782–1842) who published a series of engravings of Norfolk and Suffolk brasses in 1819. These men were interested in brasses not only as historical records, but as works of art, and as the nineteenth century progressed their number grew. Soon after the accession of Queen Victoria in 1837 brass-rubbing became a popular pastime, as contemporary accounts make clear, and by 1844 heel ball had been invented, making rubbing much easier and less messy.

It was during these years that the Gothic Revival began in earnest, because a number of factors combined to produce a revolution of taste lasting throughout Queen Victoria's reign. These included the beginnings of popular education, a renewed interest in scientific archaeology, a general demand for works of greater artistic beauty and the growing belief that art and architecture ought above all to have a moral purpose. The Cambridge Camden Society, founded in 1839, promoted fresh ideals for the reordering of churches and their worship expressive of the changes in theology advocated by the Oxford Movement. Above all, the writings of Augustus Welby Northmore Pugin injected a powerful emotional and religious drive into architectural style. Through his books the revival of Gothic art and architecture ceased to be unscholarly and became a serious pursuit.

Pugin (1812–52) (plate 2) was the son of a French refugee who was employed by the architect John Nash. He studied architecture in his father's office, and showed early on that he had a natural flair for architectural drawing and design. In 1836 he first came to the public's notice with the publication of his book *Contrasts,* which dramatically expressed his belief that the prevailing taste in architecture was decayed compared with the pure architecture of the Middle Ages. Seven years later in *An Apology for the Revival of Pointed or Christian Architecture in England* (1843) Pugin hotly attacked the cur-rent form of the sepulchral monument. 'There is not, in fact, the least practical difficulty in reviving at the present time consistent and Christian monuments for all classes of persons, and at the same cost now bestowed on pagan abominations, which disfigure both the consecrated enclosure which surrounds the church, and the interior of the sacred building itself.' He was referring to the kind of monumental sculpture prevalent before 1840. The scene was domin-ated by a few great sculptors in the Classical style, the Westmacotts,

Joseph Nollekens, James Wyatt, Sir Francis Chantrey and John Flaxman. Many of their designs are today considered superb, but to Pugin it was all pagan rubbish. The design of many monuments had become increasingly conformed and duplicated as popular designs by well-known sculptors were copied or adapted. In the pose and attitude of the figures there was a strong appeal to sentiment, which was predominantly secular in tone, and, not unnaturally, the Gothic Revivalists reacted strongly against such monuments:

> Surely the cross must be the most appropriate emblem on the tombs of those who profess to believe in God crucified for the redemption of man: and it is almost incredible, that while the dead are interred in consecrated ground, and in the ancient position – prayers for their souls' repose acknowledged to be of apostolical antiquity, and the office recited at their interment composed from the ancient ritual – the types of all modern sepulchral monuments should be essentially pagan: and urns, broken pillars, extinguished lamps, inverted torches and sarcophagi should have been substituted for recumbent effigies, angels, and emblems of mercy and redemption (Pugin, *Apology*, p. 37).

The *Ecclesiologist* (the journal of the Cambridge Camden Society which was renamed the Ecclesiological Society in 1846) summarised in January 1845 the approved forms of monument under eight headings:

1 Sculptured coffin-stones
2 Recumbent effigies
3 Plain and low sepulchral recesses
4 Brasses and incised slabs
5 Canopied mural tombs
6 High tombs
7 Floor crosses and Lombardic slabs
8 Sunken effigies

After describing the beauties of the low sepulchral recess and the recumbent effigy, the writer goes on to say:

> We believe that brasses are the most fitting kind of monument that, under general circumstances, could be adopted. When we consider that their cost would not exceed, and seldom equal, that of mural

3

tablets, we shall think it strange indeed that a positive and most unsightly disfigurement should so long have been universally preferred to one of the greatest ornaments which a church can possess. There may indeed be at present a difficulty in procuring them of correct execution, and reasonable cost, though we shall always be glad to give information how this may be done: but a general demand for them would immediately produce the requisite supply. (We have seen some excellent brasses furnished by the Messrs. Waller of London. One large double brass, with canopies and legend, cost £60: another a floriated cross, with calvary and legend, cost £15. We take this opportunity of informing our readers that these gentlemen have made arrangements for making monumental brasses to any size and degree of richness). How to adapt our modern dresses to the severe and plain lines of the ancient gravers, would readily be learned from the suggestions thrown out by Mr Pugin on this subject.

These 'suggestions' are contained in the section on 'sepulchral memorials' in his *Apology*, in which Pugin sets out his ideas on the design of modern brasses. Pugin begins by saying that one of the principal reasons for sculptors using classical costume in the past was the feeling that modern dress was unsightly. He suggests that most people sufficiently important to warrant an effigy would be entitled to wear robes and insignia of some sort, which would produce a dignified effect. 'To represent persons of the present century in the costume of the fourteenth, is little less inconsistent than to envelope them in the Roman toga.'

After mentioning that modern female costume is well adapted for sepulchral brasses, and giving three illustrations (plate 3) of its use, he proceeds to set out in detail the appropriate costume for the different classes of clergy and civilians. Clergy could without diffi-culty use the vestments which they have traditionally worn, or be represented by a cross, with pastoral staff, chalice, book or other emblems by the side. Civilians are divided into royalty, the nobility, judges, heralds, doctors of medicine and music, aldermen, and private gentlemen for whom 'a long cloak, disposed in severe folds, would produce a solemn effect.' 'For the humbler classes', he con-cludes, 'a cross, with the instruments of their trades or crafts, with marks and devices, would be sufficient and appropriate.'

As well as his examples of female dress, Pugin's comments are illustrated with drawings of two brasses he designed. Both were made by John Hardman & Co. of Birmingham. The brass to Lady Gertrude Fitz-Patrick (1841) from Grafton Underwood, Northants. (plate 4) shows her kneeling under an elaborate canopy, with a scroll issuing from her mouth and an inscription at the foot. That to Dame Margaret Sarah Morris (d. 1842) which lies in Marlow RC church, Bucks., consists of a cross fleury, at the foot of which is a lamb with the cross and banner. In the centre of the slab, on the right of the cross, is a shield and coat-of-arms round which is the motto of the Order of the Bath, 'Tria Juncta in Uno'. At the foot of the cross is an inscription recording that Catherine Gladell Vernon placed this as a memorial to her sister. At each corner are the emblems of the Evangelists, and there is a border inscription which reads:

> Dame Margaretta Sarah Morris / widow of Vice Admiral Sir
> James Nicoll Morris Knight Commander of the Bath / daughter of
> Thomas Sommers Cocks and Anne his wife a daughter of
> Alexander Thistlethwaite / Died XIIIth Jan in the year of our
> Lord God MDCCCXLII.

These two brasses are typical products of the collaboration between Pugin and John Hardman's Birmingham metalworking firm, which will be examined in the next chapter.

The earliest piece of evidence for Pugin's involvement in brass engraving is his small Gothic brass in memory of his first wife, Anne. She died in 1832, and the brass was probably engraved within the next few years. Beautifully lettered and set in a black marble slab, it lies in the north aisle of Christ Church Priory, Hants.

However Pugin was not alone in reviving the art of brass engraving. The other contestants for that distinction are Messrs J. G. and L. A. B. Waller and J. W. Archer.

John Wykeham Archer (1808–64) was a steel and wood engraver who turned his hand to brass engraving in 1839. In several lectures given at the time and reported in the *Builder*, the Society of Arts *Transactions*, and elsewhere, Archer stated that, 'In July 1839 I had the opportunity of reviving the use of church brasses', adding that 'In producing these works I have met with assistance and encouragement from members of the Cambridge and Oxford Camden Societies, and Clergymen and gentlemen of taste.'

5

Archer bases his claim on a brass he made for Dr Martin Davy (1763–1839) (plate 5), now in the ante-chapel of Gonville and Caius College chapel at Cambridge, which he describes as 'the first attempt towards the revival of the use of sepulchral brasses'. This Archer describes as 'a small brass' including an effigy of Dr Davy in a niche composed of the representation of one of the gates of Gonville and Caius College, called the Gate of Honour. It is now inlaid in the pavement of the chapel. The style of both design and execution is somewhat debased.

However, Archer, by repeated self-praise and recommendation was soon asked to carry out other commissions for brasses, two at least in Cambridgeshire, one in Worcestershire and another for India. By 1848 he claimed to have produced 'upwards of 20 brasses, chiefly of my own design'. Some are described in his various talks; another example is in St Mary's church, Fowlmere, Cambs. – a rather poor cross on a slim stem within a marginal inscription in raised black-letter showing all the signs of being etched, rather than engraved. It dates from 1843 (plate 6).

At Wargrave, Berks., Archer laid down a large brass covering a space of 9 feet, inlaid in Purbeck stone, and consisting of the figure of an angel with a sword lowered, on which is inscribed 'The sword of the spirit, which is the sword of God'. In the angel's raised hand there is a chalice with a label inscribed 'I am the way'. Two lesser figures support a diapered drapery bearing the legend. This monument was dedicated by the Enniskillen Dragoons to their officer, Colonel White. After a fire in 1914 which destroyed the church, only the subsidiary figures and inscription still exist.

Archer's repeatedly published boasts eventually proved too much for the other claimants – Messrs Waller of London, whose work was certainly far superior to Archer's. Following a long report of a talk by Archer in which he described his 'revived brasses' in the *Builder* for 4 March 1848, a polite but pointed letter appeared the following week signed by J. G. and L. A. B. Waller. Dated 11 March 1848 it reads:

Sir,

We were somewhat surprised to see in the Builder of Saturday, the 4th inst., an account of the revival of ornamental brasses, by Mr Archer, written in a manner which would lead to an inference that he alone had conduced to such an end. Now this is far from being the case, for if the merit of their re-introduction belong to any, it must certainly be ascribed to Messrs. Hardman of Birmingham (under the direction of Mr Pugin) by whom a greater number have been executed. And that we may claim some share in the matter will be allowed from the fact of our having executed nearly forty brasses, amongst which are many effigies, with canopies etc. Mr Archer's first brass at Caius College cannot be called a revival, as it is scarcely more than a large etching, and not in the spirit of the 'olden time'.

We are, Sir
J. G. and L. A. B. Waller.

The two brothers, John Green Waller (1813–1905) (plate 7) and Lionel Askew Bedingfield Waller (1816–99) are probably best known for their publication of the fine *Series of Monumental Brasses from the 13th to the 16th century*, issued between 1842 and 1864. J. G. Waller attained considerable fame in both artistic and antiquarian circles. He helped to establish the London and Middlesex Archaeological Association, he was an honorary member of the Essex and Surrey Archaeological Society, and was instrumental in helping to found the British Archaeological Association in 1844 with Albert Way and Charles Roach Smith. The Wallers did much stained glass designing and it may well have been a combination of this with their antiquarian interests that led them to become interested in the reproduction and later design of brasses.

We have seen, on the evidence of their letter about Archer, that by 1848 they had executed nearly forty brasses, and that they claimed some part in the revival of the use of monumental brasses. By the time that Herbert Haines published his list of modern brasses in 1861 they had executed over eighty, including an elaborate brass which they exhibited at the Great Exhibition in 1851, reputed to be worth £1,000 (plate 11).

Most of the Waller brasses bear the firm's trademark and as well as showing a 'family' likeness are often strikingly similar to medieval designs. Indeed Victorian writers were aware of this, as a comment at the end of a long review of current literature on brasses in the *Gentleman's Magazine* for 1848 shows: 'In the revivals of Pugin and

7

Messrs. Waller, ancient examples had been principally copied.' The Wallers were stung into replying:

> This is not so in either case. Many that we have executed are quite unlike any old examples, and even those founded on old existing types are much modified and altered from the originals; but it has often happened that we have been instructed to copy or imitate certain well known examples, but in no case has a servile copy been made (*Gentleman's Magazine*, 1849, part 1, p. 2).

The Editor, conceding and welcoming their claim, continues with the following comment, which sounds remarkably like a 'crib' from A. W. N. Pugin's *Apology for the Revival of Pointed or Christian Architecture*:

> We see no reason why monumental figures should not be designed in becoming contemporary costume, and quietly placed in modest and reverent attitudes . . . rather than have them carved in postures unsuited to a church, and either attired in 'drapery' unmeaning in itself, or in a costume which is not of their own age, and therefore of no historical value. We have no doubt that these opinions are, in a great measure, those of Messrs. Waller and we shall be happy to see many works of theirs conceived in this manner. Hitherto we have not had that pleasure.

Most of the Waller brasses are in modern dress, and if some are not, then that was usually the client calling the tune, and not the engraver or designer. On the whole their products are well executed, well designed and some of the best examples of the revived use of memorial brasses that can be found (plates 8–14).

Plate 1

BISHOP RALPH WALPOLE, d.
1301, brass engraved c.
1755, formerly in the cloister
at Strawberry Hill,
Middlesex and now in
private possession.
Horace Walpole had the
brass engraved by Johann
Heinrich Muntz (1727–98),
a Swiss painter who worked
for him between 1754 and
1759. It is based on the brass
to Robert Waldeby,
Archbishop of York, d. 1397,
in Westminster Abbey.
The inscription is as follows:

Orate pro anima Radulphi
Walpole / quondam
Episcopi Eliensis qui obiit
vicesimo secundo die mensis
martii. anno gratiae /
Millesimo trecentesimo
primi / Cuius animae et
omnium fidelium
Defunctorum propitietur
Deus Amen Amen Amen.

30 by 11¾

9

Plate 2
AUGUSTUS WELBY NORTHMORE PUGIN (1812–52) in early manhood. A portrait drawn from recollection by Joseph Nash, and published as a lithograph in Benjamin Ferrey's *Recollections of A. N. Welby Pugin* (1861), frontispiece.

+ EXAMPLES OF MODERN COSTVME ADAPTED TO SEPVLCHRAL BRASSES

Plate 3
Examples of modern costume designed by A. W. N. PUGIN, from his *Apology for the Revival of Pointed or Christian Architecture in England* (1843).
In this book he says 'modern female costume is well-adapted for sepulchral brasses.'
It is not known whether any of these designs were ever used for an actual brass.

Plate 4

THE HON. LADY GERTRUDE
FITZ-PATRICK, d. 1841, St
James, Grafton Underwood,
Northants.

One of Pugin's earliest and
best designs in the medieval
style. Set in a slab of black
marble on a low table tomb
in the north chapel, the brass
was made by John Hardman
& Co., Birmingham. An
engraving of it appears in
Pugin's book *An Apology for
the Revival of Pointed or
Christian Architecture in
England* (1843).
Lady Fitz-Patrick was the
daughter of John, Earl of
Upper Ossory, and wife of
Richard Wilson Fitz-Patrick
of Farming Woods,
Northants., who had the
brass made to her memory.
Height: 82

SAPIENTIÆ

M. S
MARTINI. DAVY. S.T.P. R.S. A.S. ET. L.S.S
RECTORIS. DE. COTTENHAM. ET. IN. ECCLESIA. CATHEDRALI. CICESTRIÆ. PRESENDARII
HVIVS. COLLEGII. PER. ANNOS. SEX. ET. TRIGINTA. CVSTODIS. DESIDERATISSIMI
PATRONI. SVI. SVCCESSORIBVS. MVNIFICENTISSIMI
QVI. AB. ANTIQVA. PROSAPIA. IN. AGRO. NORFOLCIENSI. ORIVNDVS
A.S. MD. CC. LXII.
INTRA. HOS. PARIETES. SENEX. OBIIT. A.S. MD. CCC. XXXIX
SINGVLOS. IN. MEDICINA. GRADVS. JAM. ADEPTVS
DEINDE. SANCTAM. THEOLOGIAM. PROFESSVS
IN. PHILOSOPHIA. ET. HVMANIORIBVS. LITTERIS. A. LAVDATIS. LAVDATVS
AMOREM. SIBI. OMNIVM. CONCILIAVIT
VXOREM. HABVIT. ANNAM. STEVENSON
GVLIELMI. ET. MARIÆ. STEVENSON. EX. BIANA. IN. AGRO. STAFFORDIENSI
FILIAM. NATV. MAXIMAM

Plate 5
THE REV. MARTIN DAVY, d. 1839, Gonville and Caius College chapel, Cambridge.
Dr Davy stands under an arch which was copied from the Gate of Honour in the college. It
was engraved by John Wykeham Archer and was described by him as 'the first attempt
towards the revival of the use of sepulchral brasses'.
Height of figure: 17

Plate 6

ANNA MARIA BLACKBURNE, d.
1842, Fowlmere, Cambs.,
chancel floor.
A floriated cross set within a
marginal inscription in
raised letters. In the centre of
the cross is the IHS
monogram on a background
of quatrefoils. The foot of the
cross rests on four steps, and
foliage springs from the stem
of the cross. At the four
corners of the inscription are
shields. The inscription
reads:

In Memory of Anna Maria
Blackburne the beloved Wife
of / Jonathan Blackburne
Clerk M.A. & eldest
daughter of William
Metcalfe Clerk Rector of
Foulmire who departed this
life on the vth day of
November A.D.
MDCCCXLII & of her age
XXVII / leaving an infant
son Thomas William, who
departed this life / on the
IVth day of Sepr A.D.
MDCCCXLIII aged one
year & three Weeks.

The brass was engraved by
J. W. Archer, and is set in a
black marble slab.
87 by 37

Plate 7
JOHN GREEN WALLER, FSA (1813–1905).
He was an artist, antiquary and brass engraver. He was born and brought up in Suffolk
with his brother Lionel; he entered the Royal Academy Schools, and became a specialist in
designing painted glass and memorial brasses. He never married, and died at Blackheath
aged 92.

Plate 8

THE REV. CHRISTOPHER PARKINS, d. 1843, and wife ANNE, d. 1825, Gresford, Denbighs.
It is described in the papers of the Oxford Society for the Promoting of the Study of Gothic
Architecture as follows:

A large brass, executed by Messrs. Waller of London, remarkable as exhibiting the facility
with which modern costume, especially of the clergy, may be adapted to monumental
brasses. It is in imitation of the style of the 14th century, representing the two figures under
a double canopy, in that over the male figure is the monogram Ihc, over the female Mcy.
The male is in clerical habit, surplice, hood, stole and bands with a scroll 'In the day of
Judgement' which is continued in another proceeding from the female figure, 'Good Lord
deliver us'. William Trevor Parkins, who commissioned this brass from the Wallers in
memory of his parents, joined the Oxford Soc. for Promoting Study of Gothic Monuments
(Oxford Architectural Society) as an undergraduate and was an ardent exponent of the
Gothic revival. A rubbing of the new brass was presented to the Society on Nov. 13th 1844,
and he declared that the Society would be able to judge 'how far Mr Waller has succeeded
in attaining the high spirit of the old masters'.

The inscription is as follows:

Here lieth Christopher Parkins sometime Curate of this / Church who died in the year of
our Lord God M D CCC xliii / Also Anne Arabella Boscawen wife of the abovenamed
Christopher / Parkins who died in the year of our Lord God M D CCC xxx.

It is set in a polished slate slab on a low table tomb in the Trevor chapel.
78 by 30

✠ Here lieth Christopher Patkins sometime Curate of this Church who died in the year of our lord God M·D·CCC xlix. Also Anne Arabella Boscawen wife of the abovenamed Christopher Patkins who died in the year of our lord God M·D·CCC xlv·

Plate 9

GEORGE BASEVI, d. 1845, Ely Cathedral, north ambulatory.
The architect stands in contemporary dress, holding a long rule, and the ground plan of his masterpiece, the Fitzwilliam Museum, Cambridge, under a Gothic canopy in which are a T-square, dividers, and the initials GB. The canopy is decorated with naturalistic crockets and finial, and there is a decorative background of vine leaves and tendrils. The marginal inscription, which is badly worn, describes how Basevi died as a result of a fall from scaffolding under the tower of Ely Cathedral which he was in the process of restoring. Basevi (born 1794) became a pupil of Sir John Soane in 1810, and entered the Royal Academy Schools in 1813. Between 1825 and 1840 he superintended the building of houses in Belgrave Square, London. He helped to design the Conservative Club and was working on the Carlton Club's new premises in Pall Mall when he met his death. The brass is a dignified composition which still retains much of its original colour. It is signed with the monogram of the Waller brothers.
78 by 29

THE REV. and MRS WILLIAM CROSS, d. 1827 and 1849, Grimsagh, Lancs.

A huge brass in the Flemish style showing two figures under a double canopy with a super-canopy above containing allegorical figures representing Justice and Mercy, together with subsidiary figures on the pinacles of the canopy-shafts. There is a diapered background of foliage, shields at the top of the slab and a marginal inscription surrounding the composition. The monument was erected by Mr Cross's four sons, and was made by the Wallers. Their mark appears at the base of the central canopy shaft. It bears a family resemblance to the Waller and Basevi brasses (plates 11 and 9).

95 by 50

HERE LIE THE REMAINS OF WILLIAM CROSS ESQ. BORN 27 JULY 1771 DIED 9 JUNE 1827. ALSO THE REMAINS OF ELLEN HIS WIFE BORN IN DEC 1783 DIED 27 JAN 1849.

THEIR FOUR SONS ERECTED THIS MONUMENT

THEY HAD RESPECT VNTO THE RECOMPENCE OF THE REWARD. HEBREWS XI.26.

Plate 11

The WALLER brass, engraved c. 1850, Pitt House Schools, Torquay, Devon.
This magnificent brass was made for the Great Exhibition of 1851 by the Wallers, and subsequently used as a memorial to the engravers' mother, sister and a friend, Sara Hornby. Under the canopy of 'enriched pointed architecture' is a female figure with a greyhound at her feet. In the side-shafts are subjects from the six works of mercy, based on Matthew 25: 35–6, and in the centre of the canopy is a representation of the Good Samaritan. The canopy closely resembles that of the brass to Sir Hugh Hastings, 1347, at Elsing, Norfolk.

There is a fillet inscription on which is engraved: 'Hoc monumentum Johannes Green Waller Amicus Filius Frater fecit et dedicavit Gulielmus frater incidit ad dei gloriam et in piam memoriam Sara Hornby necnon Susanna Waller et Maria Filia eius.' The brass is in poor condition, and the enamel has flaked and disappeared in many places.

106 by 40

Plate 12

JANE GILBERTSON, d. 1810, Llangynfelyn, Cards.
This is an attractive composition, in which the deceased kneels with head veiled, at a
prayer desk. The lines of the figure are filled with black pigment, while the tracery of the
desk is in green and blue, and the cushion is in red. The treatment of the drapery is similar
to that of the Gresford brass (plate 8). The inscription reads: 'Here lieth Jane the beloved
wife of William Cobb Gilbertson esquire / of this parish who died the first day of May AD
M D ccc x aged xli years'. The brass, which bears the Waller mark, is set in a stone slab in
the north wall of the sanctuary.
36 by 30

Plate 13

RICHARD BAGOT, Bishop of
Bath and Wells, d. 1854,
Wells Cathedral.
A floriated cross on a long
stem with at the foot a lamb
with a cross and banner. The
whole stands on a base of
steps inscribed with the
words 'Miserere mei Jesu'.
To the left of the cross is a
crozier, and to the right the
bishop's coat-of-arms; there
are Evangelistic symbols at
the corners, and a border
inscription which reads:

In gratia et misericordia
Dei requiescit / apud
Blithfield Co: Staff: corpus
Ricardi Episcopi Bathon:
et Wellar: / cuius
memoriae hic in
benedictione / qui obiit
xvo Maii Anno Domini
MDCCCLIV: aetat: suae
LXXII.

A product of the Waller
workshops.
Slab: 84½ by 42

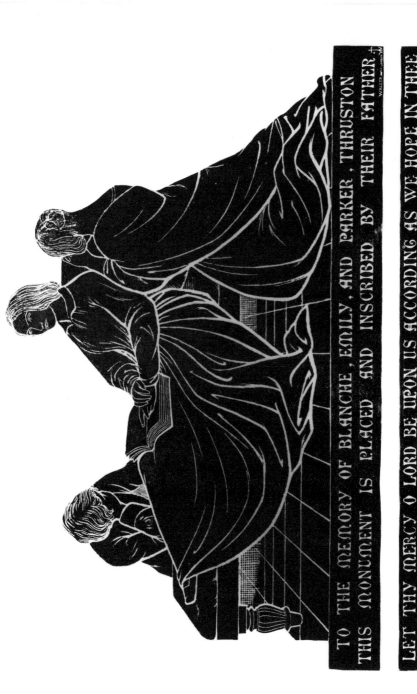

Plate 14

BLANCHE, EMILY and PARKER THRUSTON, c. 1855, Pennal church, Merioneth.

Three figures in contemporary dress, grouped naturalistically, one of the girls reclining on a *chaise longue*. There is an inscription below, and the brass is stamped 'Waller fecit London'. It is very much a Victorian conversation piece, reminiscent of the romantic three-dimensional memorials of the eighteenth century. Set in a stone slab on the north wall of the sanctuary, it commemorates the three children of Charles Thomas Thruston, Commander RN, who had married Frances Edwards, the heiress of Talgarth, Pennal.

2

PUGIN
AND THE
HARDMANS

The Hardman family originated from Lancashire, coming to Birmingham in about 1750. One of them, John Hardman, born in 1767, entered into partnership with a Mr Lewis as buttonmaker and medallist in Paradise Street in Birmingham. John Hardman was a very generous and a very devout Catholic, using his money and connections to help the building of St Chad's Cathedral in Birmingham before he died in 1844. His funeral was reported to have been attended with the greatest solemnity the Roman Catholics of Birmingham had dared to exhibit since the Reformation. His son, John Hardman junior (1811–67) (plate 15), was a partner with his father for many years in the buttonmaking industry, and in 1837 met Augustus Welby Northmore Pugin at Oscott College, a Roman Catholic public school and seminary just outside Birmingham, which was being rebuilt by an architect named Joseph Potter of Lichfield. As a result of Pugin's visit to Oscott, and probably his comments as well, Potter was dismissed, and Pugin installed as supervisory architect. At the end of the year he was lecturing to the Oscott students and providing John Hardman with drawings and designs for every conceivable aspect of metalwork. The two men had become close friends by this time and in 1838, John Hardman junior established, with Pugin as a partner, a new medieval metalworking business with the knowledge and workshops available to manufacture all kinds of ecclesiastical metalwork and church fittings. Hardman did not leave the family button business in Paradise Street when he set himself up as a medieval metalworker, and the firm of Hardman & Iliffe took part in the Great Exhibition of 1851. It was only in 1845 that John Hardman was able to gather together all the craftsmen working in the medieval metalworks in a single establishment in Great Charles Street in Birmingham. Hardman appears from the first to have used the long-standing Paradise Street factory for his 'medieval' work, so that it was the other activities he had begun, encouraged by Pugin, such as stone-carving, wood-carving and leatherworking, that had had to be carried out elsewhere in the city by outworkers until these new premises were acquired. The metalwork business began very modestly in 1838, the earliest objects produced being small in size and chiefly of precious metals – hanging lamps, candlesticks, chalices, flagons, metal mountings for books and so on. On these objects Pugin lavished much care and attention, scrutinising each stage of the processes through which they passed. The business grew, until by 1849 the gross value of the orders received totalled about £14,500, of which Pugin received a percentage, as the designs were his and he acted as an agent for the firm. Much of the inventory was made up of stock patterns to which Pugin was continually adding, designing articles specifically for sale to the general public. Pugin and Hardman were by now operating a large-scale business in mass-produced metalwork, and Hardman must therefore have had considerable managerial ability. Pugin's drawings also show that he well understood the technical aspects of manufacture, and the construction of medieval objects. He lived in Ramsgate and produced drawings there, being in constant daily touch with Hardman in Birmingham, where he would occasionally appear to consult about problems of manufacture or design, but by and large the firm's affairs were carried on by letter. The production of monumental brasses was merely one aspect of the metalwork factory's vast output. We know that Pugin prepared designs for brasses in accordance with his Gothic principles both from the illustrations in his *Apology*, and also from his designs and other records remaining in the possession of the Birmingham City Museum and Library. About 1845, some letters survive from Pugin to Hardman which bring to light the more human side of Pugin, as well as the pressures under which he was working at that time. They concern a brass to Edward Wallis (plate 16), in St John's Wood church, London: the first is from Pugin to Hardman, dated 7 August:

The price of the brass for St. John's Wood is altogether £30. Out of this I want £3 for the designs and Myers will want £2 for fixing. I've kept the cross and so forth simple. It is small and I think worth £25 clear to you. You will perceive that there is very little detail in it and the figures are easily done.

So far, everything was satisfactory. The next is from William Powell junior to Hardman:

Nothing can be simpler than the brass question if that Reverend Mr O'Neill [the priest in charge] told Myers before the brass was begun that the slab was to be white, and this done to fit an arch. Now Myers must be made to pay for letting the brass into a slab of that description. He is the most stupid blundering man in some things, though so clever in others, that I ever knew.

And Pugin to Hardman again, late 1845:

I have received the enclosed rigmarole about that wretched brass. It appears that humbug Myers forgot all about the marble and the shape of the head when he told me about the brass, and the only way to do it is to get a new slab and let it in, and I must share the loss with you. It will be a lesson to me in the future. I'm furious. I feel half inclined to kick the thing out and leave the hole.

The Myers mentioned was George Myers, a builder who worked with Pugin on many occasions. Another letter to Hardman from Pugin complains about the pirating of his designs:

I do not think this plan of sending sketches to people good. I know I make quantities of sketches of brasses which I send, then they get other people to work for them. Where are all those grand brasses under canopies which I sketched?

That gives some idea of what the man was like. Meanwhile, the volume of work coming to Pugin and the Hardmans was enormous, and though it was easy for Hardman simply to employ more workmen to keep up with the demand, the vast majority of the designs still came from Pugin himself, in metalwork, glass, furniture, fabrics, wallpaper, sculpture, stone and wall painting. He was also scrupulous in his attention to detail, as the following quotation from a letter to Hardman of July 1845 shows. It concerns a brass to a Mrs Knight, formerly in St Mary's (RC), Cadogan Street, London. Pugin re-marks: 'Mrs. Knight on the brass must be represented with a double chin – this I must draw out. You will see her age etc. in the last table.' In the Birmingham Museum there is a rubbing of that brass, which shows Mrs Knight kneeling before a floriated cross, within the head of which is an Agnus Dei (plate 17). A close-up of Mrs Knight's figure reveals that Pugin's instructions were faithfully carried out – she is resplendent with double chin (plate 18)! The Hardman Order Books show that the brass was let into a blue stone slab, measuring 6ft 6in by 3ft at a cost of £47.

This fastidious attention to minute detail eventually took its toll. After a while Pugin's health began to suffer and by 1846 he was seriously ill, though the flow of clients, and therefore designs, did not cease. In 1849 the results of his early work with Hardman in the metalwork field were publicly shown at a Birmingham exhibition and two years later at the Crystal Palace; the medieval court was a feast of his designs and Hardman's skilled labour, but it was also his last public appearance, because a bitter attack in the *Rambler*, a Catholic journal, on Pugin's designs and aims, signalled a steady decline in his popularity. Myers was constantly looking for new jobs and Hardman was panicking as he felt that his business was threatened. In 1851 Pugin was very ill and the next year he was placed in a mental hospital where he died in September. Pugin's death could have been a considerable blow to the Hardmans, though it must have been long expected, but John Hardman Powell who had been at one time Pugin's pupil and apprentice, and who was also by this time his son-in-law, took over the artistic direction of both the metalwork and the glass departments. He was also responsible for the firm moving to its new premises in New Hall Hill in Birmingham, where it remained for the next 120 years. John Hardman junior took into partnership his nephews, William Powell, James Powell and John Hardman Powell. He died in 1867 and was buried at St Mary's convent, Handsworth, Birmingham, where he is commemorated by an attractive brass showing him kneeling in an elegant cloak with a scroll surrounding his head, on which is a line of musical notation (plate 19). His son, John Bernard Hardman, who had been educated at Oscott and the Catholic University of Dublin, succeeded him. He became a partner almost immediately after his father's death, and kept up the standard and character of the firm's work very successfully indeed. In 1883 the two branches of the business were again split up, the glassworks remaining in New Hall Hill, while the metalworks were removed to King Edward's Road, and these were now renamed Hardman, Powell & Company. John Bernard died in 1903 and is commemorated by two brasses, one in Oscott College, and a second one in St Chad's Cathedral. He in turn was succeeded by his sons, John Tarlton and Gerald Hardman, who split the business between them, Gerald taking the metalwork side and John Tarlton being left with the glass business until he in turn retired in 1935. This split had been their father's idea, although it was understood between them that monumental brasses should be common ground to both. By the 1920s the demand for metalwork was low, and any brasses ordered were designed in the stained glass works which was still in New Hall Hill.

A vast accumulation of the firm's records survives, consisting of drawings, sketches, rubbings, correspondence and ledgers, which are now housed in the Birmingham Reference Library and Museum. From these it is possible to trace the designing and making of a brass from the first request by the client, through the various changes of design, including questions about size and type of slab, even mistakes made by Hardmans and their clients, until the finished product is placed in the church. A random selection from one of the ledgers shows the final cost of this lengthy process.

August 25th 1841:
N. Hopkinson, Esq.,

	£	s	d
Monumental Brass Engraving	36	10	
Stone Slab and Setting	1	10	
Screws and Burrs		10	
Mr. Pugin for drawing and superintendence	1	18	6
Box and Packing	1	1	
	41	9	6

October 17th 1842:
Rev. H. R. Harrison

	£	s	d
A Monumental Brass in memory of W. B. Darwin Esq., with coat of arms in Zinc and Colour Stone on complete	39	10	0
Packing and Case		14	0
	40	4	0

October 13th 1843:
Mrs. Amherst

	£	s	d
An Iron Tabernackle lined with silk	3	5	0
A small Monumental Brass	7	0	0
Setting into Slab Box and Packing –	3	14	0
A large Monumental Brass	23	10	0
Setting into Slab Box and Packing –	8	13	0
	46	2	–

September 23rd 1844:
A. W. Pugin, Esq.

	£		
Lyme: A Monumental Brass to drawing for Sutton Esq.,	23	–	–
Setting into Slab –	12	–	–
	35	–	–

October 4th 1844:

	£	s	d
Albury: H. Drummond Esq. 3 Monumental Brasses to drawings Boxes	150	–	–
	150	–	–

December 7th
J. D. Coleridge, Esq.
Oxford

	£	s	d
A large Monumental Brass Let into Blk Marble full length	100	–	–
effigy under a canopy and inscriptions Boxes and packing	1	10	–
	101	10	–

It is interesting to note the difference in price between a small and a large brass, which could vary from £7 to £100, depending on the elaboration of the design and the size of the slab. Each brass would have been carefully packed and boxed to be sent to its required destination, and the appropriate figures entered in the ledger in beautiful copperplate script.

Amongst many names the register mentions three monumental brasses made for H. Drummond, Esq., costing £150. These still survive, and form part of an interesting collection, worth examining in greater detail.

Henry Drummond (1786–1860) was owner of the Albury estate, near Guildford, Surrey, and was Member of Parliament for West Surrey from 1847 until his death. He hired Pugin to add a funerary chapel to the little church in Albury Park, probably in 1839, although the work was not completed until 1847. The Drummond chantry is one of Pugin's most successful works, combining his stained glass, tiles, brasses, sculpture and carving in a pleasing harmony. There are six brasses there including one on Drummond's own tomb chest which stands on a platform beneath the great south window. All are to members of the Drummond family and are in the form of crosses of varying elaboration, with inscriptions, shields and evangelistic symbols (plate 20). They are unfortunately in a bad state of repair, and a few bits are already missing.

Another example of Hardman's work is the brass to Sophia Sheppard (d. 1848) in Holy Trinity, Theale, Berks. (plate 21). Mrs Sheppard, who was sister to Dr Routh, the extremely long-lived President of Magdalen College, Oxford, gave money for the church, old rectory and school to be built. The church is a fine early Gothic building, the first to be built in England in reasonably accurate Early English style. Sophia Sheppard's brass lies on a cenotaph which is enclosed in William of Wayneflete's chantry (transferred to Theale in 1830 by the gift of Dr Routh).

While this brass clearly draws its inspiration from medieval examples, it could hardly be mistaken for a medieval memorial. The favoured metalworkers of the ecclesiological movement subscribed to the rejection of machinery and the use of medieval techniques, although it is obvious from looking at Victorian metalwork that they generally produced work that had a glossy and mechanical finish. A large ecclesiastical metalworking firm such as Hardmans turned out many hundreds of brass plates, many of them with figures, and could not possibly have used medieval techniques without considerable adaptation. An example of the way in which the pressure of business led to the use of stock patterns is given by two rubbings in the collection of the Birmingham Museum. The first is to the Rev. Thomas Sherburne (plate 22). He has a rectangular brass, on which is engraved a figure in mass vestments (scrupulously following Pugin's suggestions set out in his *Apology*), standing under a canopy with an angel at either side holding a scroll and an inscription beneath. The Order Book mentions a black marble slab and a price of £77. However, another rubbing, this time to the Rev. John Ignatius Lecuona, who died in February 1855, reveals an almost identical design, stroke for stroke, except for some minor alterations (plate 23). The inscription is obviously different, the writing on the right hand scroll is reversed, and the priest's head is now on a cushion. These two memorials show that Hardmans were using stock patterns, probably adapting the hundreds of designs left to them by Pugin.

A catalogue of Hardmans' Medieval Metalwork of c. 1875 in the Victoria and Albert Museum confirms the impression that they were by then offering stock sizes and designs 'off the peg' to their customers. Two pages of memorial brasses offer the purchaser a choice of slab or plate alone and every conceivable permutation of size and price. Brasses were being mass-produced on a scale reminiscent of the later Middle Ages. Alongside these standard designs, however, Hardmans continued to offer special designs if the client so wished. Indeed the examples of their work illustrated in plates 28–42 show a remarkable variety, ranging from the elaborate and costly brass to Sir Charles Barry (plate 28) to the diminutive inscription plates to Annette and Lewis Peniston (plate 42). Many of their designs also show great technical ability and assurance, such as the two large canopied brasses in St Augustine's Abbey, Ramsgate (plates 29 and 30) and that to George Elkington from Selly Oak, Birmingham (plate 36). Others are more remarkable for their curiosity, in particular the Rev. John Wheble (plate 34), Mrs. Ellen Berington (plate 41) and First Lieutenant W. E. K. Cockell (plate 38). All reveal that Hardmans paid great attention to detail, and would take endless trouble to ensure that the finished product was satisfactory. The vast correspondence in the Birmingham Reference Library frequently bears this out.

At St Mary's College, Oscott, near Birmingham, there is an amazing collection of nearly fifty brasses grouped together on a single wall in one of the side chapels (plates 24–7). Their story is an interesting example of Hardmans' continuing involvement with one client over a period of about sixty years.

St Mary's College was established as a Roman Catholic seminary, and at one time boarding school, during the 1830s as a replacement for the college built at Old Oscott some forty years earlier. The chapel, the main body of which was completed in 1838, incorporates several side chapels to the south-west, including the Weedall chantry, which was erected in memory of Henry Weedall, the first president of the re-founded college, who died in 1859. All the brasses may be found in the side chapels, and some forty-four are fixed to a single wall in the chantry, having the locations indicated on the plan in plate 27.

It was in 1867 that the Very Rev. J. S. Northcote, who was then president of the college, proposed to the Oscotian Society, one of whose objects was 'the material improvement of portions of the chapel', that it should lend its support to the idea of a memorial to past members of the society, in the form of a Mortuary Tree of brasses. Such a monument was to consist of a wall in the Weedall chantry painted with patterns of foliage so contrived as to represent the Tree of Life, and at the same time to depict geometrically a relationship between the brasses in their relative positions on the wall and on the Tree. In this way, therefore, the brasses to former presidents were to be concentrated at the centre of the wall – the trunk of the Tree – whereas those to persons less intimately connected with the college were to be positioned on the lines or branches emanating from the trunk. The society subsequently approved such a plan, and the first brasses for the Tree, to college presidents, were formally ordered by Canon Northcote towards the end of 1868, the decoration of the wall having been completed the previous year.

A description of this Mortuary Tree is given in *A Catalogue of pictures, wood carvings, manuscripts and other works of art and antiquity* published for St Mary's College, Oscott in 1880, and compiled by the Rev. William Greaney; it runs as follows:

Item 343

THE FRESCO on the wall (of the Weedall Chantry) represents THE ANGEL OF DEATH STANDING ON A TOMB, from which springs the Tree of Life, and on the branches of this tree hang memorial brasses, recording the obits of alumni of the College. This decoration was done at the expense of the Oscotian Society, 1867.

Item 344

The following are the names and obits on the brasses to the present date:
Cardinal Wiseman, 1865; Monsignor Weedall, 1859; Dr. Moore, 1856; Dr. Morgan, 1861; Rev. Michael Drewe, 1850; Everard A. de Lisle Phillipps, 1857; Canon Flanagan, 1865; Edward J. Spencer Northcote, 1865; Canon Richmond, 1867; Maurice Welman, 1867; Colonel Bennett, 1867; Charles J. Powell, 1867; Rev. Charles Pearson, 1868; Rev. Walter Martin, 1869; Osmund C. Phillipps de Lisle, 1869; Alfred A. Z. Palmer, 1870; Charles Jefferies, 1870; John J. D'Arcy, 1874; James A. Dease, 1874; David (error for Henry) Lamb, 1878; Rev. Daniel H. Haigh, 1879.

In this fashion, brasses were positioned on the wall until the turn of the century, when the Tree began to lose its significance, and brasses were then placed in locations which destroyed its former geometric precision and symmetry (plate 25). At some time after this, when the last brasses had been laid down, the whole wall was painted over, and it was only recently that a considerable amount of restoration work was done. During this, the brasses were re-waxed, and thoroughly cleaned, though of the original painted Tree there is still no sign. A photograph in the Benjamin Stone Collection of Photographs in the Birmingham Reference Library, 'Confessional and Side Chapel in the Church at Oscott College, Warwickshire, 1879' (Box 39, Photo 40), shows the wall and the 'Mortuary Tree' as it then was (plate 24).

The original Tree was to the design of William Powell, the cousin of John Bernard Hardman. Hardmans engraved all the brasses laid down at the college, and were also responsible for a large amount of the stained glass there. From Hardmans' ledgers, order books and day books the dates at which all these brasses were ordered can be ascertained, together with a great deal of information about the Tree contained in correspondence between the society and Hardmans. Sketches were submitted by Hardmans to Dr Northcote during 1867, only to be returned with suggestions for alterations. Eventually at a meeting of the Oscotian Society in November 1867:

> Mr Powell's design for the mural decoration . . . after a short discussion received its approval. It was proposed and seconded that it should be submitted to the General Meeting in Midsummer to devote £50 towards erecting tablets and the mural decoration to the four deceased presidents of the college.

Even then it was to take over a year before Hardmans were able to produce the four brasses. Indeed in November 1868 Hardmans had a letter from Dr Northcote as follows:

> *Dear Sirs,*
> We are quite in despair of getting any designs for the brasses for the former presidents from Mr. John Hardman Powell and think of having our own device executed by the village blacksmith!

Finally, though, all was well, and the way in which the brasses have since proliferated over the wall can be seen in the modern photograph of the chapel (plate 26). It is a quite remarkable series, and but for some clever detective work might have lain undiscovered for ever.

Hardmans carried on through the Second World War producing mainly stained glass, though still designing the occasional brass, but early in 1970 a fire seriously damaged the studios in New Hall Hill. It was obvious that the firm would have to move, and in 1972 they bought a lovely eighteenth-century mansion, Lightwoods House, set in spacious grounds three miles from the centre of Birmingham, from where they still carry on the business of designing and making stained glass.

Plate 15
JOHN HARDMAN (1811–67), from a portrait photograph taken in 1838 when, with Pugin, he founded Hardman's metalworking firm. The picture hangs in the studios of John Hardman & Co., now at Lightwoods House, Birmingham.

Inscription on the brass (as shown in the image):

✠ Pray for Edward ... Wallis, Esq. he died
Janᵉ xxu. Mdccccxliw ... aged lxx years.
On whose soul may ... God have mercy

Plate 16
EDWARD WALLIS, d. 1844,
St John's Wood,
London.
A crucifix with at its base
a representation of the
deceased kneeling in
prayer, and on either side
of the crucifix the Virgin
Mary and St John.
Beneath them is the
inscription and below
that a shield of arms.
This brass, made by
Hardmans, is referred to
in Pugin's
correspondence because
of difficulties over setting
it into its black marble
slab.
47 by 25

Plate 17

MRS MARY KNIGHT, d.
1845, formerly in St
Mary's Cadogan Street,
London (RC).
A cross fleury, with an
Agnus Dei within it, to
which Mrs Knight
kneels, holding her
missal and rosary. There
is an inscription
underneath and
Evangelistic symbols at
the four corners.
Designed by Pugin and
made by Hardmans.
Set in a blue stone slab.
78 by 36

Plate 18
Detail from the brass to MRS MARY KNIGHT, showing her double chin, which Pugin was so anxious not to miss out! An example of an attempt at portraiture on revived brasses.

Plate 19
JOHN HARDMAN, d. 1867, St Mary's convent, Handsworth, Birmingham.
A kneeling figure in a cloak with a scroll on which are the words 'Domine dilexi decorem domus tuae et locum habitationis gloriae tuae' with a plainsong tune above them. The inscription shows an interesting mixture of Gothic black-letter and Lombardic script. The brass was made by Hardmans of Birmingham, and represents the founder of the firm and a great friend of Pugin.
25 by 15

Plate 20

LADY HENRIETTA DRUMMOND,
d. 1854, St Peter and St Paul,
Albury, Surrey.
A very elaborate cross with
an Agnus Dei at the foot,
scrolls, shields of arms and
an inscription. It lies in the
Drummond chantry chapel
which Pugin designed. The
Hardman registers reveal
that the brass, set in its black
marble slab, cost £50. Other
brasses to members of the
Drummond family also lie in
the chapel.
78 by 36

Plate 21

MRS SOPHIA SHEPPARD, d. 1848, Holy Trinity church, Theale, Berks.

This fine brass, designed by Pugin and made by John Hardman & Co., lies on a table tomb enclosed by the chantry chapel of William of Wayneflete, who founded Magdalen College, Oxford, in 1458. The shrine was transferred to Theale in 1830 as the gift of the Rev. Dr Martin Routh, the long-lived President of Magdalen, who was Sophia Sheppard's brother. Dr Routh was the first rector of Theale, and his sister was the wife of a later rector, Thomas Sheppard DD. She had built, at her own expense, the church, old rectory and school, and it was through her efforts that Theale became a separate parish. The church, designed by E. W. Garbett of Reading, has been described by Sir John Betjeman as 'the first church in England to be built in reasonably accurate Early English Revival style'.

Mrs Sheppard's brass consists of a figure with inscription beneath. She is shown dressed as a widow, with a dog sitting at her feet. The lines are boldly drawn, and the overall effect is one of severe simplicity. The inscription reads:

M S
Sophiae Sheppard
Huius Ecclesiae Fundatricis
Quae Obiit
Die xxxi Julii
A S
MDCCCXLviii,
Aetatis suae
LXXX

Height: 46

Plate 22

THE REV. THOMAS SHERBURNE, brass ordered 1856, provenance unknown.

A rectangular plate showing the figure in eucharistic vestments under a canopy supported on each side by angels carrying scrolls, below each of which is an ornamental shield with device upon it. The initial letters in the right hand shield can be paralleled in Pugin's *Glossary of Ecclesiastical Ornament*, where they appear as part of a design for an altar frontal. The inscription records that he founded the church of St John the Evangelist. This brass is an almost exact duplicate of one to the Rev. John Ignatius Lecuona. The Hardman Order Book for 1855–7 contains details of this brass, although no information about where it was erected. Both this and the Lecuona brass were copied from the brass to the Rev. Michael Crewe, Stowbridge (RC) church, which had been ordered in 1850.

Black marble slab: 36 by 24

✠ Orate pro anima Thomæ Sherburne, Sacerdotis
huius Ecclesiæ fundatoris sub titulo S. Joannis Evang.
consecratæ pridie festi S. Georgii A. D. Mdcccxlv. R.I.P.

Plate 23

THE REV. JOHN IGNATIUS LECUONA, d. 1855. A similar composition to that to the Rev. Thomas Sherburne, showing that Hardmans must have had stock patterns to offer their clients, which could be varied in small ways to suit the individual's taste. Hardman's Order Book for 1855–7 states that the 'architect' was W. W. Wardell Esq., The Green Hill, Hampstead, and that when completed the brass was to be sent to the Rev. John Kaye, Catholic Church, Triangle, Hackney, London. The inscription reads:

Hic jacet servus Dei Joannes Ignatius Lecuona, / Sacerdos, Fundator hujus Ecclesiae eiusque primus Rector. / Natus die sexto Junii Mdcccvi. Obiit die vigesimo octavo / Februarii Mdccclv. Cuius animae propitietur Deus. Amen.

Black marble slab: 36 by 24

Hic jacet servus Dei Joannes Ignatius Liervona.
Sacerdos Fundator huius Ecclesiæ, eiusque primus Rector
Natus die sexto Junii Mdcccvi. Obiit die vigesimo octavo
Februarii Mdccclv. Cuius animæ propitietur Deus. Amen.

Plate 24
An early photograph of the interior of the Weedall chantry, St Mary's College, Oscott,
Birmingham, showing the fresco on the wall, representing the Tree of Life on which hang
memorial brasses recording the deaths of members of the college. Behind the curtained
statue of the Virgin Mary was a representation of the Angel of Death, standing on a tomb.
Photograph c. 1897 from the Benjamin Stone Collection in the Birmingham Reference
Library (Box 39, photo 40).

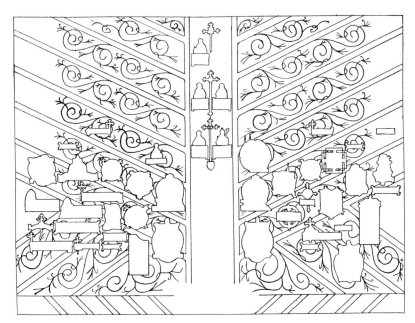

Plate 25
A reconstruction of the painted Mortuary Tree, Oscott College, Birmingham, showing
the fresco covering the wall and the brasses hanging from the 'branches'. The blank space
at the base was originally filled by a representation of the Angel of Death standing on a
tomb.

Plate 26

A modern view of the Weedall chantry, Oscott College, Birmingham, showing the wall covered in memorial brasses, but with the fresco obliterated. The Mortuary Tree is a unique idea, and only old records in the college, and the vast Hardman deposit in the Birmingham Art Gallery and Reference Library have brought it to light.

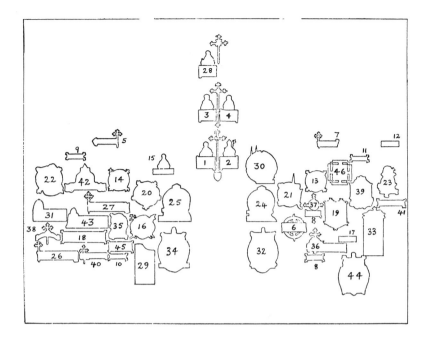

Plate 27

Key to the Mortuary Tree, St Mary's College, Oscott, Birmingham. The drawing shows the brasses as they appear on the wall today.

1 Henry Weedall, 1st President of Oscott College, 1859: demi-figure in mass vestments with chalice, inscription underneath.
2 Nicholas Wiseman, 2nd President, Cardinal Archbishop of Westminster, 1865: demi-figure in pontificals, inscription underneath.
3 John Moore, 4th President, 1856: demi-figure in mass vestments.
4 George Morgan, 5th President, 1861: demi-figure in cope.
5 Edward Joseph Spencer Northcote, 1865: inscription on scroll.
6 George Bennett, 1867: inscription encircling sword and belt.
7 Charles James Powell 1867: inscription on scroll.

All the above engraved in 1868

8 Thomas Flanagan, 1865: inscription.
9 Maurice Welman: inscription.
10 Henry Richmond, 1867: inscription.
11 Charles Pearson, 1868: inscription.

All the above engraved in 1869

12 Alfred Augustine Zouch Palmer: inscription on scroll.
13 Everard Aloysius de Lisle Phillips, VC, 1857: kneeling figure in cassock and gown with Victoria Cross, holding sword.
14 Osmund Charles Phillips de Lisle: kneeling figure in cassock and surplice.
15 Walter Martin, 1869: demi-figure in mass vestments holding chalice and wafer.
16 Charles Jeffries: figure in cassock seated at reading desk, before angel with scroll.

All the above engraved in 1870

17 Michael Crewe, 1850: inscription on scroll, engr. 1874.
18 James Arthur Dease, 1874: inscription, engr. 1875.
19 John Joseph D'Arcy, 1874: figure in cassock reclining on couch.
20 Henry Lamb, 1878: figure in cassock seated at writing desk with books, inkpen, etc., engr. 1879.
21 Daniel H. Haigh: kneeling figure in mass vestments at prayer desk, church in background, engr. 1879.
22 James Brown, 1881: kneeling figure in cope and mitre beside St James the Great, engr. 1882.
23 Charles Meynell: demi-figure of St Charles of Borromeo, with lilies and monogram, engr. 1882.
24 Francis Kerrill Amherst: coped figure kneeling before Cardinal Wiseman, engr. 1883.
25 Rudolph Bagnall: coped figure kneeling while another celebrates mass before an altar, engr. 1883.
26 George Mostyn, 6th Baron Vaux of Harrowden: inscription and cross, engr. 1883.
27 George Charles Mostyn, 1879: inscription and cross, engr. 1884.
28 Henry Logan, 3rd President of College, 1884: half-effigy in gown with cross, engr. 1885.
29 Eustace Zouch Palmer, 1890: figure in cassock standing beneath tower ringing angelus bell, engr. 1891.
30 William Morgan Stone, 1890: priest in cope standing at eagle lectern with saints, angels, etc., engr. 1891.
31 William Grosvenor, 1891: figure in mass vestments kneeling at an altar, engr. 1892.
32 Edward Howard, Cardinal Archbishop, 1892: figure in pontificals kneeling under canopy before Pope Pius IX, with part view of St Peter's, Rome, engr. 1894.
33 Francis Frederick Withers, 1898: figure standing under canopy at eagle lectern.
34 Edward Charles Acton, 1899: figure kneeling before the Virgin Mary, engr. 1900.
35 Vincent Ormsby Holcroft, 1899: figure standing at desk and holding open book and chalice, engr. 1900.
36 Lieut. Gen. the Hon. Sir James Charlemagne Dormer, 1893: inscription on scroll, engr. 1902.
37 John Bernard Hardman, 1903: floriated cross and inscription, engr. 1904.
38 Michael Sherston Baker, 1905: floriated cross and inscription, engr. 1906.
39 William Leigh, 1906: kneeling figure at prayer desk, with seated effigy of Dr Wiseman.
40 Stephen J. Whitty, 1905: inscription on scroll, engr. 1907.
41 Henry Norris, 1906: inscription, engr. 1907.
42 John Hawksford, 1905: demi-figure of St John the Evangelist, engr. 1908.
43 Major-General Victor Edward Law, 1910: figure in ceremonial dress with cloak kneeling to the Virgin Mary.
44 Hon. Edmund Stonor, 1912: kneeling figure at prayer-desk under canopy, engr. 1913.
45 Henry Edward Rhind, 1899: inscription, engr. 1913.
46 William Greany, 1907: inscription and ornamental cross, engr. 1922.
Note: The numbering on this key is not the same as that in the revised Mill Stephenson List of Monumental Brasses for Warwickshire, published by the Monumental Brass Society in 1977. Fuller details of all the brasses will be found there.

Plate 28

SIR CHARLES BARRY, d. 1860,
nave, Westminster Abbey,
London.

The memorial consists of a
cross bearing
representations of the
Paschal Lamb, symbols of
the Evangelists, roses,
leaves, the letter 'B', and a
portcullis, all set between an
elevation of the Victoria
Tower of the Houses of
Parliament which Barry
designed, and the ground
plan of the Palace of
Westminster. Underneath is
an inscription, and
surrounding the whole
composition is a border fillet
lettered with the words of
Colossians 3: 23–4. At each
corner there is the letter B in
a quatrefoil.

An anonymous writer in the
Athenaeum for 13 August 1864
commented:

The departure from the
character of the erected
tower which is marked in the
elevation in question with
regard to the entrance, is, we
presume, a sort of protest on
behalf of the deceased that
his design was meddled
with!

The brass was made by
Hardmans of Birmingham
at a cost of £700.
97 by 43

Plate 29

THE REV. ALFRED LUCK, d.
1864, St Augustine's Abbey,
Ramsgate, Kent.
He is shown in full
eucharistic vestments
standing under an elaborate
canopy with his head
pillowed on a cushion, and at
his feet an inscription. There
is also a marginal inscription
with Evangelistic symbols at
the corners. Luck was an
Oblate of the Order of St
Benedict, and one of the
founders of St Augustine's
monastery. He became a
priest after the death of his
wife, and both his sons
joined the monastery.
The brass was made by
Hardmans of Birmingham.
88 by 42

Plate 30

DOM WILFRED ALCOCK, d.
1882, St Augustine's Abbey,
Ramsgate, Kent.
Another product of the
Hardman workshops, lying
in the north cloister of the
abbey, before the altar which
is a memorial to him. He
died and was buried in New
Zealand. He wears a cope
and mitre and carries a
crozier.
Slab: 90 by 34

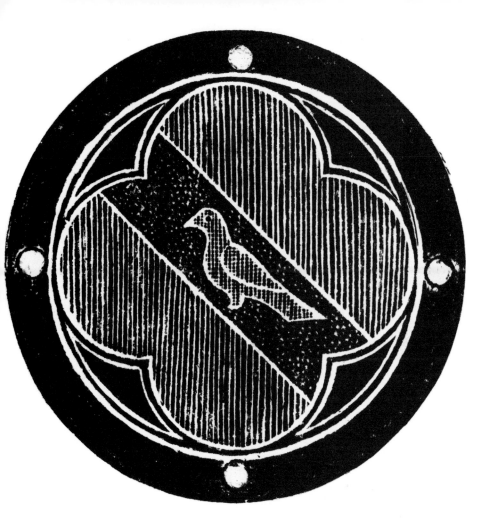

Plate 31

Roundel from slab covering the PUGIN family vault, St Augustine's Abbey, Ramsgate, Kent.

An example of the minute attention to detail typical of Pugin's splendid church are the brass roundels which conceal rings on the vault cover in the nave floor. They are nicely engraved with the Pugin arms (gules, a band or) and the family emblem, the 'temple haunting martlet' (*Macbeth* I: v: 3) which also appears on his tomb, and on the Minton floor tiles of the Pugin chantry.

Diameter: 6

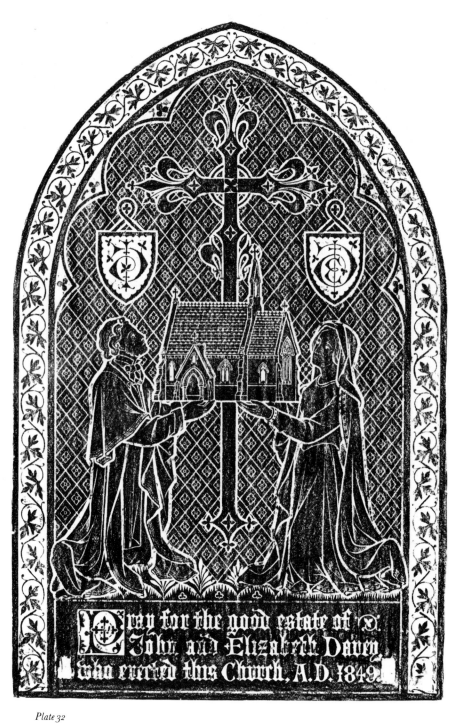

Plate 32

JOHN and ELIZABETH DAVEY, 1849, St Birinus (RC), Dorchester, Oxon.
An arch-shaped brass showing two figures kneeling to a cross and holding a model of the church they helped to build. There is a patterned background and border. The design and lettering are particularly good. It is set in a black marble slab.
30 by 21

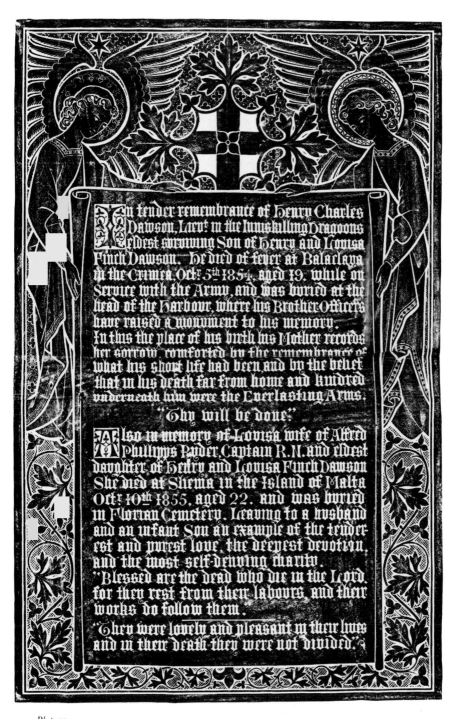

Plate 33

LIEUTENANT HENRY CHARLES DAWSON, d. 1854, provenance unknown.

Two angels hold up a scroll on which is the inscription. There is a cross fleury at the top.
Dawson died, aged 19, of fever at Balaclava. The monument is also a memorial to his sister,
Louisa. It is a well-engraved brass with dignified lettering.

28½ by 18½

Plate 34

THE REV. JOHN J. WHEBLE, d. 1854, formerly in St George's Cathedral (RC), Southwark, London.

An attractive and ornate composition, showing Wheble kneeling in eucharistic vestments in front of an ornamental background and beneath an elaborate single canopy with a roundel showing chalice and wafer. Beneath his feet is a panel showing him giving the last rites to dying Catholic soldiers at Balaclava, where he died. There is a border inscription with a verse from Psalm 23. Made by Hardmans of Birmingham.

49 by 22

Plate 35
ROBERT STEPHENSON, d.
1859, nave, Westminster
Abbey, London.
Stephenson is represented in
contemporary dress, with his
arms folded across his chest.
The figure is set into a slab
with fleurs-de-lys cut in low
relief within a lettered
border. At each corner is a
quatrefoil enclosing a
floriated cross.
Unfortunately the figure
gives the impression of
floating on its back.
The brass was designed by
Sir Gilbert Scott and made
by Hardmans of
Birmingham.
Stephenson was President of
the Institution of Civil
Engineers.
92⅛ by 43½

Plate 36
GEORGE RICHARDS
ELKINGTON of
Woodbrooke, 1865, and
wife, MARY AUSTER, St
Mary, Selly Oak,
Birmingham.
Two kneeling figures,
with scrolls, under a
double canopy,
surmounted by a
floriated cross. Now
mural, in the chancel.
Engraved by John
Hardman of
Birmingham. An
attractive brass, finely
engraved, although both
figures are facing out of
the composition, giving it
a lop-sided look.
69¼ by 34¼

Of your Charity pray for the
Souls of the deceased and for the
Good Estate of the living members of the
Fulford family Benefactors of this Church

Plate 37
The FULFORD family, c. 1845, mural, nave, St Osberg's (RC), Coventry.
A crucifixion with an inscription to members of the Fulford family, benefactors
of the church.
Almost certainly a product of Hardmans of Birmingham.
Height: 34

Plate 38

FIRST LIEUTENANT WILLIAM EDWARD K. COCKELL, d. 1866, Newtown, Newbury, Berks.
A rectangular plate showing a representation of the Stilling of the Storm by Jesus (Luke 8: 22–5), below which is the inscription recording that Cockell served on HMS *Rattler*, and fought in China for many years, seeing action at Fatshan and Canton and dying at Penang. The whole composition is surrounded by an ornamental border, and is very unusual. Made by Hardmans of Birmingham.
27 by 21

Plate 39

THE REV. WILLIAM JOHN BEAMONT, d.
1868, Trinity College chapel,
Cambridge.
A figure in cassock, surplice, scarf
and stole, with stock and buckled
boots, standing on a grassy mound.
His head is pillowed on a cushion,
and there is a scroll above his head
which reads:

Christ shall be magnified in my
body whether it be by life or by
death. Phil. 1.20.

Beneath Beamont's feet is the
inscription:

In memory of William John
Beamont / Senior Fellow of this
College & Vicar of St / Michael's
who fell asleep in the Lord Aug⁴ 6
1868.

Beamont was a Fellow of Trinity
from 1852 and travelled widely,
visiting the Crimea and the Holy
Land, where he met Holman Hunt.
In 1858 he founded the Cambridge
School of Art. He is also
commemorated by a stained glass
window in St Michael's church,
Cambridge.
The brass was designed by Alfred
Waterhouse (1830–1905) and made
by Hardmans at a cost of £83.
Slab: 96 by 39, height of
composition: 82

Plate 40
THE HON. ARTHUR FREDERICK EGERTON, d. 1866, Worsley, Manchester.
A striking plate, showing against a patterned background, a cross fleury, and two angels
holding an inscription scroll. Below this is a separate plate with a verse from scripture
'Weep not for the dead / neither bemoan them for / they are at rest'.
Both are set in Caen stone.
46 by 26

Plate 41

MRS ELLEN MARY BERINGTON, d. 1866, possibly in Boulogne, France.
She was a Franciscan Tertiary, and is depicted kneeling before a crucifixion, with a long
scroll which reads: 'I thank Thee O my God: for having given me a life of trial and
disappointment.' Two winged angels hold chalices which catch the blood from Christ's
wounds, and a third chalice is engraved at the foot of the cross. Opposite the figure of the
lady is a shield showing the cross with two arms crossed in front of it and nailed to the
cross-beam. Below is the inscription.

Hardman's Order Book for 1865–6 notes that this brass was 'fixed' with another which
was to be restored at the same time, to William Berington, d. 1847, in Little Malvern
church. Charles Berington of Little Malvern Court, Worcs., placed the order in October
1866. The Order Book states that Mrs Berington's brass was to be sent to . . . .
church, Boulogne. No doubt this happened, although further details are not recorded in
the Order Book.

Black marble slab: 12⅝ by 11⅛

Plate 42
ANNETTE and LEWIS PENISTON, babies aged 4 and 7 months, who died in 1872 and 1869
respectively. Small inscription plates wrapped around sprays of lilies, and placed on
the east wall of the Pugin chantry chapel, St Augustine's Abbey, Ramsgate, Kent.
Made by John Hardman & Co., Birmingham.
Inscriptions: 3½ by 6¾

3

LATE
VICTORIAN
BRASSES

Hardmans were so prolific in the manufacture of memorial brasses during the latter part of the nineteenth century that they seem virtually to have monopolised the field. However, by the 1860s, there were many other firms springing into prominence, and we must turn to these to complete the picture of nineteenth- and early twentieth-century brass manufacture. Below are brief details of the most important firms, together with examples of their work.

BARKENTIN & KRALL
290 Regent Street, London. Floruit 1870–1920
Founded by George Slater Barkentin and Carl Krall c. 1870. Their most famous brass is probably that to Sir George Gilbert Scott in Westminster Abbey, designed by the architect, G. E. Street (plate 44). Another in the Abbey by them is to G. E. Street, designed by Bodley (plate 43). They also made the brass to the Rev. W. S. Sanders, 1901, in St Nicholas, Guildford (plate 62) and many fine raised letter inscriptions, as well as other good figure and cross brasses.

COX, SONS, BUCKLEY & CO
28–9 Southampton Street, Strand, and College Works, Esher Street, Westminster. Floruit 1860–1916
Founded by Edward Young Cox. Made mainly brass inscriptions. The *Builder* for 13 May 1882 reports that they made a brass in the

fifteenth-century style for President James Abram Garfield (1831 –81), Republican President of the USA who was assassinated on 1 March 1881, dying from his wounds on 19 September. It consists of the grand seal of the USA, two shields on each side of a sword and a simple inscription. It was to be placed in the Episcopal Church of Elberon, next to the house where he died.

CULLETON'S HERALDIC OFFICE

92 Piccadilly; later, 25 Cranbourn Street, St Martin's Lane, WC. Floruit c. 1890
Founded in the late 1880s. Advertisements in the early issues of the *Cambridge University Association of Brass Collectors Transactions* state: 'Monumental Brasses designed and engraved in medieval and other styles, and supplied ready for fixing. A speciality made of accuracy in detail and style.'

FARMER & BRINDLEY

67 Westminster Bridge Road; Hercules Buildings, London. Floruit 1850–1937
Firm established by William Farmer and Joseph Brindley. Mainly stone masons – they supplied the black marble slab for the Scott brass in Westminster Abbey, as well as for many others. Still listed in 1937 but Brindley had retired and models, photos and rubbings could be obtained from Fenning & Co. Ltd.

GEORGE T. FRIEND

Engravers, 9 Dyers Buildings, Holborn, London. Floruit 1920–78
This firm of engravers was responsible for a number of figure brasses, and many inscription plates. They specialised in finely engraved lettering, and are mentioned in *Lettering* by Graily Hewitt, a teacher at the Central School of Arts and Crafts, published in 1930. They engraved the brass to Lieutenant-Colonel Bernard at Nether Winchendon, Bucks. (plate 79). Mr W. Turner, who took over the business, cut the lettering on the Hatfield Hyde inscription (plate 78), and engraved the brass to the Rev. Vivian Symons, at Biggin Hill, Kent. At the end of 1978 Mr Turner had to leave the workshop in Holborn, and the firm closed down.

T. J. GAWTHORP & SON

16 Long Acre: later 11 Tufton Street, London SW1. Floruit 1859 –1936

'Memorial Brass Engravers', founded by Thomas John Gawthorp (1832–1912). Held several royal warrants: described in 1914–18 directories as 'brass, wrought iron and repoussé workers, monumental masons and memorial engravers: art metal workers to H.M. the King'. The firm did much to repair and restore medieval brasses as well as engraving modern ones. A good example is that to Dean George Pellew (d. 1866) in Norwich Cathedral (plate 46). A catalogue of theirs in the Victoria and Albert Museum, dated 1865, gives as examples of prices, £40 for an elaborate inscription with shields, architectural work, etc., £15 for a highly ornamented floriated cross, and £10 for a plain inscription with ornamental border. Their brasses were 'made from the best metal, ⅛ in. in thickness and including the necessary fastenings'. On the back cover of the *Oxford Journal of Monumental Brasses* for December 1900 is an advertisement for Gawthorp's 'Latten Brasses', illustrated with a brass in Lowther church, Cumberland (plate 47). At some time in the mid 1880s the firm of Matthews & Sons of London amalgamated with Gawthorps.

When T. J. Gawthorp died in 1912 his son Walter Edmund Gawthorp took over. When he died in 1936, the business was taken over by Wippells.

HART & SONS, later HART & SONS, PEARD & CO

138, 140 Charing Cross Road, London and Grosvenor Works, Birmingham. Floruit 1860–1914

Founded by Charles Hart and Thomas Peard. Peard was an apprentice ironmonger who joined the firm of Hart & Son in 1853, then in 1860 set up his own business with Frederick Jackson. The two firms amalgamated c. 1867 in Birmingham. Hart's foundry is still there but old records appear to have perished. In the 1870s the architect, William Butterfield worked for them for a time. They had a showroom in Regent Street, London in 1870, and produced mainly wall plates and a few figure brasses, notably George Swan Nottage (1823–85), Lord Mayor of London, in the crypt of St Paul's Cathedral, designed by Edward Onslow Ford, RA (1852–1901) (plate

48), and William Dyce, RA (1806–64), painter and ecclesiologist, in St Leonard's, Streatham, London (plate 49). There is a catalogue of theirs in the Victoria and Albert Museum, illustrating some of their designs.

HEATON, BUTLER & BAYNE LTD

London and New York. Floruit 1857–1939
Founded in 1857 by Clement Heaton (1824–82) an ardent Gothicist, and Timothy Butler as a firm of glass painters and church decorators. Later he was joined by M. J. Bayne & Co. A catalogue in the Victoria and Albert Museum advertised their products as 'genuine latten brass – the fine old metal engraved in Flemish and afterwards in English workshops of nearly seven centuries ago, which remains today the only suitable material for memorial brasses' (c. 1917), and quotes examples for sale in New York, ranging from $90 to $1,270. Their best known memorial brass is that to the Rev. Herbert Haines (1826–72) in Gloucester Cathedral, designed by Capel N. Tripp (plate 50). They also produced a large number of wall brasses, usually signed.

JONES & WILLIS LTD

43 Great Russell Street, London. Floruit 1870–1939
Founded in Birmingham as Messrs Newton, Jones & Willis; by c. 1900 they could supply almost the entire furnishing for a church from organ cases to brasses and stained glass. They were church furnishers to Queen Victoria and published a *Book of Designs of Ecclesiastical Art*. Most of their brasses are enamelled wall plates, often with evangelistic symbols at the corners. They are usually signed. A nice figure brass is that to John Kemp, Canon of Wakefield, d. 1895, from St Peter's, Birstall, West Yorks. (plate 51).

MATTHEWS & SONS

377 Oxford Street, London. Floruit 1850–80
The name of this firm first appears in the 1850s, as on a brass dated 1852 in St George's chapel, Windsor, inscribed 'E. Matthews, London'. Matthews is also referred to in a classic paper on fixing brasses, published in 1889 by Sir Henry Dryden in the *Associated Architectural Societies' Reports and Papers*. Other examples of the firm's work are at Coleshill, Warks., 1859, Lutterworth, Leics., 1881, and a particularly fine brass to Matthew St Quintin, d. 1876 at Harpham, Yorks., with

angels, arms and inscription (plate 52). The firm evidently amalgamated with Gawthorps about 1880–90, as we find brasses signed with both names, as at Penkridge, Staffs., 1897, and Layer Marney, Essex, 1897 (plate 58).

OSBORNE & CO. LTD
7 Eastcastle Street, Oxford. Floruit 1874–1971
Makers of 'brass, bronze, copper and nickel silver memorial tablets, hand engraved, wrought in relief – carved, cast and repoussé. War memorials, rolls of honour, ecclesiastical figure brasses inlaid in floors in specially imperishable metal. Highest standard of design and craftmanship. Well designed lettering in the best old and modern styles'. A catalogue of 1938 advertises an exclusive alloy called ' "Oscraft", the nearest approximation to the metal used in the best period of medieval brasses'. Their designs for figure brasses have a distinct family likeness. Most common are standard design rectangular plates. A more elaborate design is at St Edmund's College, Ware, signed by the designer 'Herbert Wauthier', for Osbornes. An example of a figure brass designed by Wauthier is that to the Rev. Wilmot Phillips, dated 1935, Shrine of our Lady of Walsingham, Norfolk (plate 53). The firm was dissolved in 1971 when Vanpoulles of London took it over.

SCULPTURED MEMORIALS AND HEADSTONES
12 Lower Regent Street, London. Floruit 1930–40
This firm seems to have arisen in response to a demand for cemetery memorials of good design and lettering. Well-known sculptors and architects produced designs which were then mass-produced for the public at prices ranging from £10 to £50. A catalogue of 1934 states that they will supply 'well-executed memorials in stone, brass, bronze or wood, and will use local material and British labour'. They made a few brasses including that to the Rev. H. B. Hyde (d. 1932) at Denchworth, Berks., designed by Julian P. Allan, the sculptor (plate 54).

J. W. SINGER & SONS
Frome, Somerset. Floruit 1870–1926
Produced mainly wall plates with black-letter inscriptions and traditional decorative borders. In 1887 they produced what a contemporary journal described as 'one of the largest brasses that has lately

been produced in England', the memorial to the Rev. Jordan Roquette Palmer-Palmer, MA, FSA in Bristol Cathedral (plate 55). Other brasses are at Datchworth, Herts., 1877; Whitchurch Canonicorum, Dorset, 1908; Duxford, Cambs., 1918; and Piddlehinton, Dorset, 1933. The firm kept going until 1926 when the Morris-Singer Co. (now at Basingstoke) took over the business. They no longer make brass and bronze memorials.

FRANCIS SKIDMORE & SON

Meriden, Birmingham. Floruit c. 1845–70s

Francis Skidmore was the son of a Coventry watchmaker and silversmith. He was a member of the Ecclesiological Society. In 1845 he entered his mark at Birmingham Assay Office. In the early 1850s he began making plate and metalwork for outside designers, including Sir George Gilbert Scott, with whom he had a long connection. Skidmore made the brasses for the monument to Princess Mary, Duchess of Gloucester, d. 1857, in St George's Chapel, Windsor, designed by Scott, and that to the Ven. George Hodson, 1855, in Lichfield Cathedral. Another example of his work is in Holy Trinity, Coventry, to John Johnstone Hook, d. 1836 (plate 56). In 1861 he began a foundry for large base metal work, and the younger Skidmore went into partnership to form Skidmore's Art Manufacturing Company. A Birmingham firm took over the business in the mid 1870s.

J. G. & L. A. B. WALLER

20 Charles Street, and Bolsover Street, London. Floruit c. 1840–80

Because of their artistic and antiquarian interests the Waller brothers began designing in stained glass. This may have led them towards brass design, because they are mentioned in the *Ecclesiologist* of January 1845, as having arranged for brasses of varying size and richness to be made. From 1842 they were at 20 Charles Street, Middlesex Hospital, but by 1872 they had moved to Bolsover Street, where they remained for many years. Their products are distinctive and nearly always bear their trademark, often including the words 'Waller Fecit'. The Wallers also repaired and restored brasses, as at Lingfield in Surrey, and St David's Cathedral, Pembs. Good examples of their own designs are those to George Basevi, 1845, Ely Cathedral (plate 9) and Bishop Bagot, 1854, Wells Cathedral (plate 13).

J. WIPPELL & CO
London and Exeter. Floruit c. 1900 to date
Made mostly wall plates, some with crosses, between 1900 and 1919.
Took over business and premises of Gawthorps in Long Acre in 1937.
Now Wippell-Mowbray Church Furnishing Ltd, 28 Margaret
Street, London W1 and 11 Tufton Street, London SW1.

It is only occasionally possible to get a picture of the day-to-day
business of these nineteenth-century firms. The Hardman archives
give us a revealing picture of the workings of one big firm, but there
are glimpses to be found of others. The calligrapher, Mervyn C.
Oliver, who was apprenticed to Barkentin & Krall has left a fascinat-
ing account of their Regent Street offices. He described his experience
as follows:

At the age of fourteen I was very keen to be a draughtsman,
although I understood nothing about it. One day I saw an
advertisement in one of the national dailies: 'Boy wanted with
talent for drawing'. I said to my father: 'Here's my chance; we must
go there at once' – and I went with him to an address in Regent
Street; there we saw a curious little German in a fine antique shop
filled with medieval and renaissance metalwork of all kinds, but
mostly ecclesiastical. This shop, in which I was destined to work
for six years, was a few doors from the Polytechnic, and the original
Central School of Arts and Crafts was on the opposite side of the
road in a Georgian house that had been bought by the L.C.C. It
was the close proximity of the Central School, the Polytechnic and
my job that put me on my feet. The year was 1900, the Central
School had started in 1896, and Edward Johnston had started
teaching there in 1899. I was appointed to my job for five years,
with the possibility of a further two. I started at eight o'clock in the
morning, when I unlocked the safes and did various odd jobs –
made working drawings, found others in the files, searching
through old dusty boxes and old rolls of working drawings – and in
general ran, fetched and carried between making tracings until
6.30 in the evening. I did no silversmith's work at all during my
apprenticeship; I merely drew and watched people working in the
factory whenever I was sent over there on errands; I remember in

77

particular watching the engravers. We were supplying ecclesiastical silver during the revival of church ornaments. The best architects of the day used to come in with their designs, and although they themselves had never done a piece of metalwork, they could always design a fine chalice, cross or iron screen. Their drawings, when the job was finished, were filed for further reference, and I used to turn this file over and study it carefully. I remember old Bentley, the architect for Westminster Cathedral, bringing in a drawing of a chalice which had to be made in 18 carat gold; a fine, simple design which I have never forgotten. During my last three years, Carl Krall – the partner who had come to this country from Heidelberg – was controlling the business. He was limited as a designer and is better described as an adapter. There was no such thing as an original design in the sense of it being absolutely new. Each design was merely a little different from the last or, if it came from an architect, might have been a better-proportioned adaptation. The old man was surrounded by what he had bought from dealers here and what he had collected abroad, Gothic and Renaissance antiques. We had to make careful drawings of these things for further reference, and they were then adapted or repeated when the chance came. It was a regular business of turning out metal-work from such stock designs. Occasionally there had to be a difference: a pair of candlesticks had to be made a different height, and I would then make a drawing with the addition in the same style: that was how I learned the difference between Gothic, Classic and Renaissance work.

I found Krall an exceedingly difficult man to work for, and the only praise I received from him was half a dozen grudging remarks in about six years. Naturally, I wanted to get away from Krall after my five or six years had been completed. My wages were 5s for the first year, rising to 6s 8d, 11s, 14s and 21s. I never reached 28s for the seventh year. I remember we worked from eight o'clock till 6.30 every day and eight o'clock till two o'clock on Saturdays (from John Farleigh, *The Creative Craftsman*, Bell, 1950, pp. 197–9).

It is frustrating that the records of so many of these companies have either been dispersed or destroyed. The drawings and other material of a firm like Barkentin & Krall would be invaluable, as would those of Singers, Osbornes, and Heaton, Butler & Bayne, whose records now no longer exist.

As well as the bigger manufacturers there were other smaller firms, both in London and the provinces, as well as local craftsmen, funeral masons, etc., who would perhaps only produce one or two figure or allegorical brasses and a handful of inscriptions in their lives.

Occasionally names of individual designers occur, such as William Weyer of Norwich, who designed the large brass to the Rev. W. F. Creeny (plate 59); a Mr Thomas King of Chichester, Sussex, who in 1846 was reported to be making an ecclesiastical brass of a priest, copied from a monument in Dieppe of 1447 (*J. Brit. Archaeol. Assn*, I, 1846). King appears in *Pigot's Directory* for 1839 as 'Drawing master, antiquary, medallist, artist and engraver. East St.' Where his finished brass is, if it was completed, or whether King engraved any other brasses, is not known. Possibly his work was like that of J. W. Archer. Perhaps other individual wood or metal engravers also turned their hands to brass-engraving, just as they had done in the seventeenth century and later. It was not, after all, an unnatural move.

By the end of the nineteenth century we can see a picture of proliferating numbers of metalworking firms producing mainly simple inscription plates, and a few larger brasses. However, although the total number of brass plates undoubtedly increased during the nineteenth century, the popularity of figure brasses was less predictable. A chart of figure-brass production for the nineteenth and early twentieth centuries reveals that the peak came between 1840 and 1860. There seems to have been a fall-off in numbers produced during the 1860s and 1870s, and another peak in the 1880s and 1890s. Again in the years between 1915 and 1920 there was a brief revival, and after that numbers tail off drastically.

The main reason for this fluctuation is that towards the end of the nineteenth century there was a reaction developing within artistic circles to the revived use of memorial brasses. A writer in the *Ecclesiastical Art Review* of March 1878 remarked:

> During the last thirty years a large number of modern brasses have
> been placed in our churches. Opinion will differ how far they are a
> success, but to me they have always been more or less
> disappointing, though it may not be easy to give any good reason
> for this.

He goes on to say that the fault lies not in the attempt to represent modern dress on brasses, but rather in three smaller areas:

1 the filling of the engraved lines with black mastic;
2 the placing of brasses on highly polished marble;
3 the failure to compete in beauty with the altar-tomb and its recumbent effigies.

And the writer continues:

> But, after all, it is very questionable whether it would be desirable to restore the use of brasses to any large extent. In some churches where there is room on the floors to place them without fear of their being subject to the wear and tear of feet, they might well be used: and in churches we should be glad to see the usual style of mural monuments replaced by brasses simply let into the wall. . . . But the brass never can be an architectural decoration. It must always be treated as a memorial.

This decline in popularity is well illustrated by an incident during a meeting of the Chapter of Lincoln Cathedral. When Canon Edmund Venables, Precentor at the time, tried to persuade his colleagues to commission a brass in memory of Christopher Wordsworth, Bishop of Lincoln from 1869 to 1885, the Dean asked him:

> My dear Precentor, can you seriously contemplate the prospect of people in hob-nailed boots trampling upon his saintly person?

Nothing more was heard of the brass.

Plate 43
GEORGE EDMUND STREET, d. 1881, nave, Westminster Abbey, London.
Street, wearing a college cape, is represented as kneeling before a floriated cross, with a scroll issuing from his mouth 'Domine, dilexi decorem domus tuae'. Opposite are his shield of arms, three Catherine wheels, and surrounding all is an elaborate floral border, with figures of six saints within niches formed by foliations of the vine. From the top they are St George and St Edmund, patron saints of Street; then St Thomas, the patron of builders, and St Peter, the patron saint of the abbey; finally there are St Catherine, whose wheel forms the family arms, and St Barbara, the patron saint of architects. At the four corners are Evangelistic symbols, and six Tudor roses separate the figures.
The memorial was designed by G. F. Bodley and made by Barkentin & Krall in 1884. The marble slab was supplied by Messrs Farmer & Brindley.
90⅝ by 48⅜

✠ IN ✠ MEMORY ✠ OF

George Edmund Street Architect R.A. Anno Dno

of December 1881 In the hope of eternal life

Domine dilexi decorem domus tuæ

fidelis

inter perfidos

MCC 8 III VO

Plate 44

SIR GEORGE GILBERT SCOTT, d. 1878, nave, Westminster Abbey, London.
The brass was designed by the architect, G. E. Street, who described it as follows:

The cross and border round it, the shields and inscription are all to be brass, let into a
slab of marble, which will have a carved border all round its outer edge. The inscription
will be similar to that which the coffin bore. The cross has an Agnus Dei in the centre and
the emblems of the four evangelists at the ends of the arms.

There are allegorical figures at the corners representing the painter, sculptor, smith and
carpenter, as well as shields and other devices. Sir Gilbert Scott himself is represented at
the foot of the cross, seated at his desk and studying a drawing. It is a very fine composition,
beautifully executed, with a mass of intricate detail. It was made by Barkentin & Krall.
Messrs Farmer & Brindley supplied and worked the carving on the marble. It cost about
£400 which caused a writer in the *Church Builder* of 1879 to comment:

We learn with regret that out of a little over £900 which has been paid or promised about
half the sum will be absorbed by the cost of the monumental slab, leaving less than £500
for the foundation of an art teachership, art workmen students' exhibitions, prizes, or
whatever other way of promoting the education of art-workmen might have been
considered desirable. We feel bound to say that we should, under the circumstances,
have been much better satisfied with a much less elaborate and costly design, for which
some of the simple but beautiful ancient designs would furnish suggestions.

It was laid down in 1881.
91¾ by 50¾

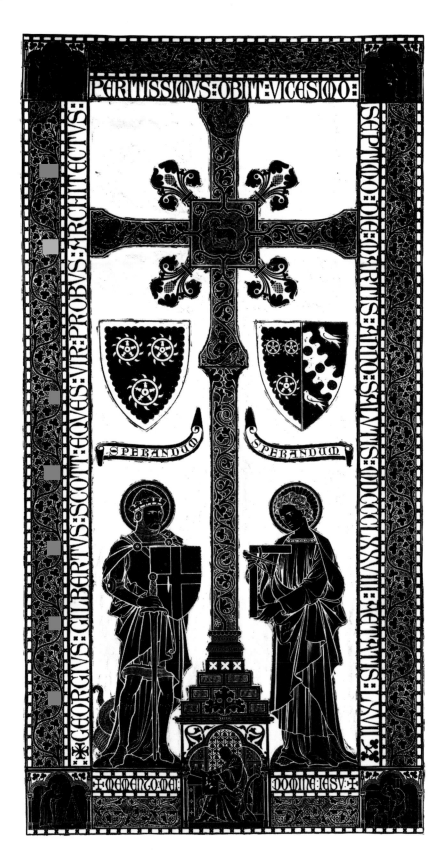

Plate 45
Portrait of SIR GEORGE GILBERT SCOTT (1811–78) from his memorial brass in Westminster Abbey (plate 44), drawn by Frank Theodore in 1910. It shows him sitting at his desk studying a plan, in his architect's robes. The face is a good likeness.

IN LOVING MEMORY OF
GEORGE PELLEW D.D. 3RD SON OF ADMIRAL VISCOUNT EXMOUTH
BORN APRIL 6 1793. DIED OCTOBER 13 1866. 17 YEARS DEAN OF THIS CATHEDRAL
FOR THE SERVICE OF WHICH HE ZEALOUSLY LABOURED
THIS TABLET IS DEDICATED BY HIS CHILDREN A.D. 1889

Plate 46

GEORGE PELLEW, Dean of Norwich, d. 1866, Norwich Cathedral.

The brass is mounted on a slab of Derbyshire fossil marble. It is engraved with the recumbent figure and portrait of the Dean within a canopy and border of stiff foliage. In addition to the inscription there are the arms of the Exmouth family and of the Dean and Chapter of the cathedral. The profile head had to be adapted from a three-quarter miniature, and is supposed to be a good likeness.

The memorial was designed and made by T. J. Gawthorp of London. It is now high up on the north wall of the nave.

42 by 64

Plate 47

An advertisement for Gawthorp's 'Latten Brasses' which appeared on the back cover of the *Oxford Journal of Monumental Brasses* for December 1900. The illustration is of the brass to HENRY, Earl of Lonsdale in Lowther church, Cumberland. The business was founded in 1859 by T. J. Gawthorp, and was eventually taken over by Wippells in 1936.

Plate 48

The RT HON. GEORGE SWAN NOTTAGE, Lord Mayor of London, d. 1885, crypt, St Paul's Cathedral, London. He is represented in his official robes, standing three-quarter length beneath a semi-circular arch, above which is the armorial achievement of the City of London. Below him is an inscription, which reads:

This Brass was placed here by / The Corporation of the City of London / in Memory of The Right Honourable / George Swan Nottage / Lord Mayor, who died during his Mayoralty, / in the forty eighth year / of the reign of Queen Victoria, / on the 11th day of April 1885, aged 62 years / and who lies buried beneath this spot.

Nottage's face, like those in most modern brasses, is intended to be a portrait. The memorial was designed by E. Onslow Ford, RA, and made by Hart, Son & Peard of London.
89 by 34½

Plate 49

WILLIAM DYCE, RA, d. 1864, St Leonard's, Streatham, London.

This large brass, designed by C. W. Cope, RA, and engraved by Hart, Son & Co., shows Dyce, palette in hand, seated in front of an easel containing one of his major works, *St John leading the Blessed Virgin from the Tomb* (now in the Tate Gallery). On the bookstand before him is an open Gospel, and in the ornamental border are representations of (on the left) St Luke, St Bennet Biscop (an Anglo-Saxon churchman), and St Cecilia, and (on the right) the Venerable Bede, King David, and St Leonard. The brass, set in a slab of slate, originally hung on the south wall of the Lady Chapel, but was badly damaged in a fire in 1975. It is hoped to raise money to restore the brass to its former glory.

William Dyce was born in Aberdeen, and gained a place at the Royal Academy. He became a devout Anglican and a leader of the High Church Movement. He decorated the walls of All Saints', Margaret Street, was interested in liturgy and church music, and was an expert on stained glass, which he both designed and executed. He established a School of Design at Somerset House in 1840. He was a prize-winner in the first of the open competitions held to find suitable artists to decorate the rebuilt Houses of Parliament, and was allotted the painting of a fresco on the subject of *The Baptism of Ethelbert* behind the throne of the House of Lords. In 1857 the Dyce family moved to Leigham Court Road in Streatham, and he became churchwarden at the parish church of St Leonard. One day in 1864 he collapsed at work and was taken home to die. It was fitting that this key figure in the Victorian art world should be commemorated by his fellow parishioners with such an interesting brass.

84 by 42

In memory of WILLIAM DYCE M.A. Royal Academician Painter Musician Scholar who died in this Parish Feb. 14. 1864 aged 57. His body rests in the Grave yard of this Church of which he was a Warden This Monument was erected by fellow parishioners & admirers of his Genius & Worth

Plate 50

THE REV. HERBERT HAINES, MA, d. 1872, south ambulatory, Gloucester Cathedral.

Haines was born in Hampstead on 1 September 1826, the seventh son of a surgeon. He was sent to school at Gloucester to study Classics, and from there he went to Exeter College, Oxford. It was during his time at Oxford that he joined the Oxford Architectural Society and began his interest in brasses. He made a catalogue of the brass rubbings in the society's collection with a long introduction by himself, which was published in 1848. From Oxford Haines went to the little parish of Delamere, ten miles north of Chester, but he found it too isolated, and in 1850 he took up the post of second master at the College School, Gloucester. He held this post until his death in 1872. It was not until 1857 that he found time to devote to the study of brasses and to revise his *Manual of Monumental Brasses*. Haines completed his *Manual* towards the end of 1860, and presented a copy to the Oxford Architectural Society. Another writer on brasses, H. W. Macklin, described the book as 'simply invaluable and no good work can be done without it'. Haines contributed other articles on brasses to various learned journals, as well as writing a handy little guidebook to Gloucester Cathedral. Shortly before the beginning of the autumn term of 1872 Haines' health suddenly deteriorated and he died after a short illness on 18 September. He appears to have left his widow in difficult circumstances, and a collection was taken for her at the College School, some of which went towards the education of the eldest son. At the same time the old boys of the College School began a fund for a memorial to Haines in the form of a brass. The Honorary Secretary of the fund was Mr Capel N. Tripp who also designed the brass. It was made by Heaton, Butler & Bayne and lies on the floor of the south ambulatory of the choir in Gloucester Cathedral. It shows Haines in cassock, surplice, stole and hood, standing under a canopy with an inscription, which translated reads as follows:

Herbert Haines MA, for twenty-three years second master of this Cathedral School, died 14 October 1872, aged 46 years, whose body lies buried in the cemetery near this city. A few of his pupils and friends, mindful of the benefits received from him, have caused this memorial to be erected.

A curious error is the date of death, which is almost a month later than the actual day. A full biography of Haines compiled by Mr Richard Busby appears as the introduction to his reprinted *Manual*, which Adams & Dart published in 1970.
76½ by 32

Plate 51

THE REV. JOHN KEMP, MA, Canon of Wakefield, d. 1895, St Peter's, Birstall, West Yorks. A rectangular plate with a three-quarter effigy cut out at the centre, showing Kemp wearing cassock, surplice and stole, and holding a prayer book. The inscription underneath and around the edge is in raised letters, and there is some nice decoration above the figure. At each corner are the four Evangelistic symbols. It is signed by Jones & Willis of London.

29 by 16½

To the Glory of God and in affectionate remembrance of John Kemp M.A. Canon of Wakefield, and of his faithful and unselfish services, this tablet was placed by members of the congregation, parishioners and friends

Curate and Vicar of this Parish
for a period of 45 years.
Born April 5th 1827
Died July 7th 1895.

Plate 52

MATTHEW ST QUINTIN, d. 1876, Harpham, Yorks.

A large rectangular plate, on which two angels with palms hold between them the inscription. Above is the achievement of arms, and at the top canopy work with an ornamental cross. At the bottom is a skull and cross-bones signifying 'death or glory'. The background is covered with oak leaves and acorns. The inscription reads:

Here is laid in faith / to rest in peace awaiting the glorious / resurrection change the mortal body of / Matthew Chitty Downes St. Quintin / second son of William Thomas St. Quintin / and Arabella Bridget his wife daughter of / General Thomas Calcraft of Grantham / in Lincolnshire. He was born 19th Dec. 1800 / at Speen near Newbury and subsequently / entered the Army serving for 27 years in / H: M: 17th Lancers from which he retired / with the rank of Colonel. He married in / 1850 Amy Elizabeth daughter of George / Henry Cherry of Denford in Berkshire / and died on 19th April 1876 leaving three / sons and one daughter.

The brass is signed 'Matthews & Sons, 377 Oxford St. London W.'
76½ by 35¾

Such as are gentle them shall He teach his ways

Here is laid in faith
to rest in peace awaiting the glorious
resurrection change the mortal body of
Matthew Chitty Downes S! Quintin
second son of William Thomas S! Quintin
and Arabella Bridget his wife daughter of
General Thomas Calcraft of Grantham
in Lincolnshire He was born 19 Dec. 1800
at Speen near Newbury and subsequently
entered the Army serving for 27 years in
H.M. 17th Lancers from which he retired
with the rank of Colonel He married in
1850 Amy Elizabeth daughter of George
Henry Cherry of Denford in Berkshire
and died on 19th April 1876 leaving three
* * sons and one daughter * *

Plate 53

THE REV. WILMOT PHILLIPS, d. 1935, Shrine of Our Lady of Walsingham, Walsingham, Norfolk.

A rectangular plate, showing a priest in eucharistic vestments of the Spanish type with his right hand raised in blessing and under a rounded arch. There is an inscription below:

Pray for the soul of
Wilmot Phillips
for 27 years parish priest of Plaxtol, Kent,
much persecuted for his faith and loyalty to the most holy sacrament: .
Born 8 May 1864 Died 27 Sept. 1935.
Jesu mercy Mary help

The brass is signed 'Wauthier Osborne London' and is similar to other products of the firm of Osbornes. In a catalogue of theirs a similar brass is described as 'executed in the medieval manner, the detail deeply and permanently incised on a sheet of "latten" brass, and inlaid flush in the church floor, the face being designed from a portrait'.

Osborne's catalogue states that the metal used for their memorials is an alloy named Oscraft, similar in kind to medieval brass, and harder than the commercial brass generally used by engravers.

The brass is somewhat baroque in its design, but is an attractive memorial.

56 by 22

PRAY FOR THE SOUL OF
WILMOT PHILLIPS
FOR 27 YEARS PARISH PRIEST OF PLAXTOL KENT
MUCH PERSECUTED FOR HIS FAITH AND LOYALTY TO THE MOST HOLY SACRAMENT
BORN 8 MAY 1864   DIED 27 SEPT 1935
JESU MERCY MARY HELP

Plate 54
THE REV. HENRY BARRY HYDE, d. 1932, Denchworth, Berks.

This brass was designed by Miss Julian P. Allan, who was also responsible for the Kendall family brass in St Mary's, Hatfield Hyde, Herts. (plate 78). It was made by Sculptured Memorials and Headstones.

17 by 12

IN LOVING MEMORY OF
HENRY BARRY HYDE
PREBENDARY OF EXETER CATHEDRAL
SOMETIME ARCHDEACON OF MADRAS
WHO DIED 12 APRIL 1932 AGED 77 YEARS

Plate 55

THE REV. JORDAN ROQUETTE PALMER-PALMER, MA, FSA, d. 1885, Bristol Cathedral, south pier of the tower.

It shows him in cassock, surplice and stole, standing under a very elaborate canopy, with super-canopy above and side-shafts, with saints in the niches. On the upper part are the figures of three angels, and the background is covered in engraving, some parts being sunk and then darkened to give effect to the bright foreground. It was designed by Mr E. S. Singer, of the firm of J. W. Singer & Sons of Frome, Somerset, who executed the work. 90 by 45

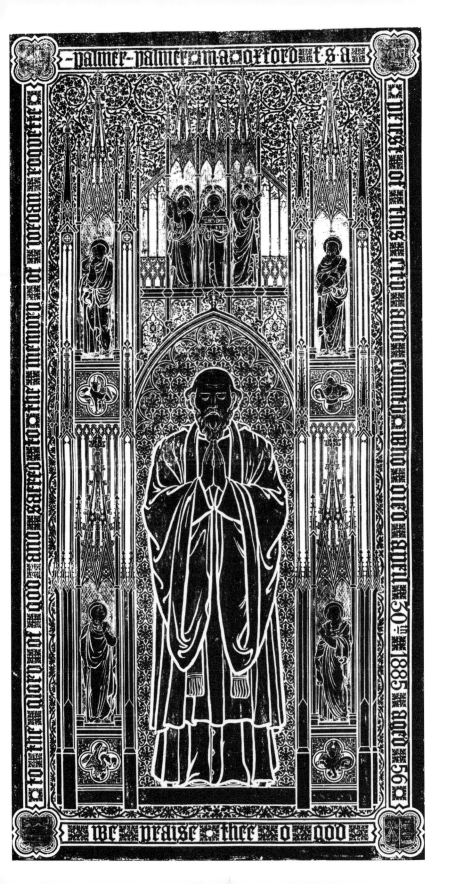

Plate 56
JOHN JOHNSTONE HOOK, d. 1836, Holy Trinity, Coventry, mural, north transept.
An ornamental cross with inscription beneath, erected in memory of the baby who died
aged 9 months, and his father, a former vicar, in 1878. It was engraved by F. A. Skidmore's
metalworking firm at Meriden, Coventry.
36½ by 21

✠ NEAR THIS SPOT REST THE REMAINS OF
JOHN JOHNSTONE HOOK WHO DIED DEC 18 1836
AGED NINE MONTHS THE SON OF WALTER FARQUHAR HOOK
SOMETIME VICAR OF THIS CHURCH
IN MEMORY OF HIM AND HIS BELOVED FATHER
THIS CROSS WAS ERECTED BY MEMBERS OF THE FAMILY 1878

Plate 57

GEORGE HAIGH, d. 1876, St Thomas and Edmund of Canterbury (RC), Erdington, Birmingham.

An inscription on a scroll held by a winged angel, the whole surrounded by a woven wreath with a rose and foliage at each corner of the slab. His widow, Josephine Haigh, provided the 'warming gear' of the church in his memory.

27½ by 27½

In Loving Memory of
Thomas Hermitage St John Boys,
Second son of Henry J. Boys,
Rector of Layer Marney,
and of Mary his wife,
who died at Rio de Janeiro, March 8th 1897
Aged 18 Years.
R.I.P

Plate 58

THOMAS HERMITAGE ST JOHN BOYS, d. 1897, Layer Marney, Essex.
He is shown kneeling before his bunk on board ship. He died at Rio de Janeiro, aged 18.
The brass is signed 'Matthews & Co. (Gawthorp) Castle St. East, W. London'.
30 by 18

Plate 59

THE REV. WILLIAM FREDERIC CREENY, d. 1897, formerly at St Michael-at-Thorn, Norwich, now in Bridewell Museum, Norwich.

Designed by W. R. Weyer, a local engraver. *Kelly's Directory of Norfolk* for 1896 describes William Robert Weyer as 'Church decorator, ecclesiastical and domestic decorations for interiors, stained glass work, heraldic artist, illuminator, designer and art tile painter. 3a Redwell Street.' By 1900 the directory includes 'memorial brass engraver, designer of art metalwork and glass embosser', and gives his address as Guildhall Chambers (Showrooms & Studios), St Peter's Street. Weyer had obviously become more successful and expanded his business.

William Frederic Creeny was not only President of the Monumental Brass Society, but also the leading authority of the time on continental brasses and incised slabs. He published *A Book of Fac-similes of Monumental Brasses on the Continent of Europe* in 1884 and in 1891 *Illustrations of Incised Slabs on the Continent of Europe.* When he died the Monumental Brass Society set up a Creeny Memorial Fund, with which his memorial brass was set up. Its design is taken from the title-page of his book on incised slabs (see plate 60), with a certain amount of modification. The brass consists of a large rectangular plate, with a finely engraved canopy, and a trefoil within which is a half-effigy of Creeny, presumably attempting a facial likeness. At the base is an elaborate screen, enclosing a shield with his canting arms – a crane followed by the letter y. At the four corners there are the four Evangelistic symbols and in the middle of the surrounding border of foliage, vine leaves, etc. are two shields.

The church of St Michael-at-Thorn was damaged by bombing during the last war and the brass suffered too. The top left-hand corner is badly buckled, making a good rubbing impossible.

69 by 45

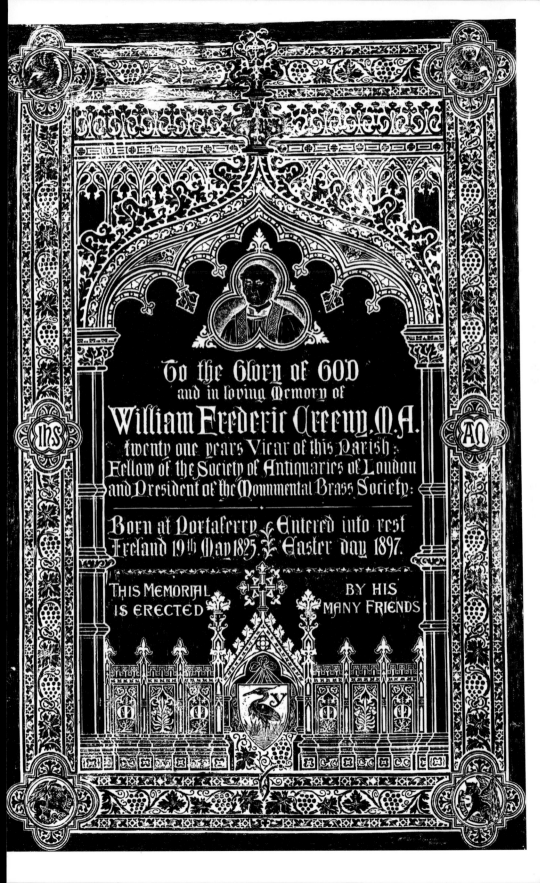

To the Glory of GOD
and in loving Memory of

William Frederic Creeny, M.A.

twenty one years Vicar of this Parish;
Fellow of the Society of Antiquaries of London
and President of the Monumental Brass Society:

Born at Portaferry ✠ Entered into rest
Ireland 19th May 1825. ✠ Easter Day 1897.

THIS MEMORIAL   BY HIS
IS ERECTED   MANY FRIENDS

Plate 60
Title-page of *Illustrations of Incised Slabs on the Continent of Europe*, published in 1891, by W. F. Creeny. The design of his brass (plate 59) bears a striking resemblance to it, and William Weyer may well have based his design for the brass upon it.

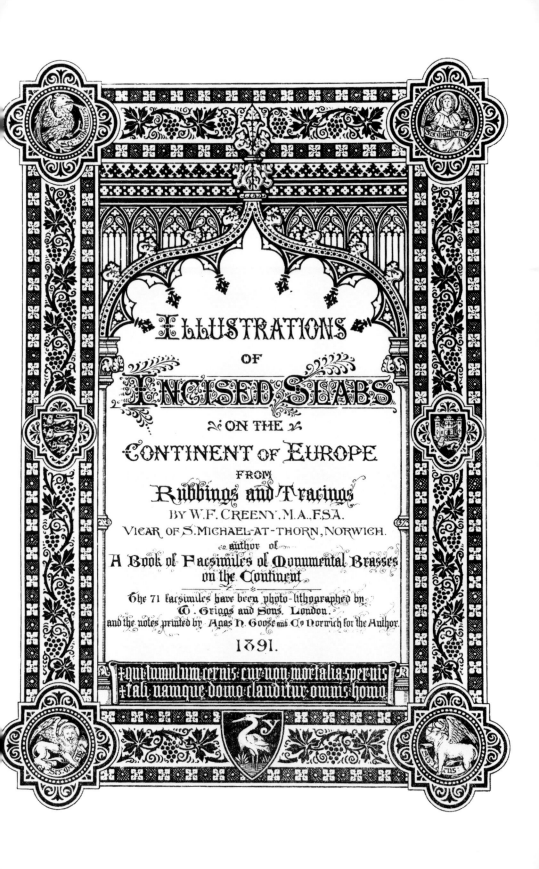

Illustrations

OF

Incised Slabs

❧ ON THE ❧

Continent of Europe

FROM

Rubbings and Tracings

BY W.F. CREENY, M.A., F.S.A.

VICAR OF S. MICHAEL-AT-THORN, NORWICH.

❧ author of ❧

A Book of Facsimiles of Monumental Brasses on the Continent

The 71 facsimiles have been photo-lithographed by
T. Griggs and Sons, London,
and the notes printed by Agas H. Goose and Co Norwich for the Author.

1891.

4

THE
TWENTIETH
CENTURY

In spite of their decline in popularity the turn of the century saw some really fine brasses laid down, such as those in St Mary Magdalene, Paddington (plate 61), St Nicholas, Guildford (plate 62), and St Peter's, Hascombe in Surrey (plate 67). There is a delightful miniature brass in Little Bardfield Church, Essex (plate 66), and another attractive memorial to the Rev. T. C. Skarratt, at Kemsing, Kent (plate 68). The Boer War and First World War also produced a number of pleasing brasses, as at Birchanger and Marks Tey in Essex (plates 63, 71) and numerous regimental memorials.

However, many of the older brass engraving firms were by now beginning to die out, and the techniques and skills of the old engravers were dying with them. One firm that spanned the turn of the century and continued until the 1930s was Gawthorps.

On T. J. Gawthorp's death, his son, Walter Edmund Gawthorp, took over. He had entered the firm in 1875, and took great interest in both ancient and modern brasses. He was a member of the Monumental Brass Society and contributed regular articles to their *Transactions* and those of other societies. Amongst these are 'Restoration of Ancient Brasses' in *Notes and Queries*; 'Ancient and Modern Methods of Engraving Brasses' in the *Transactions of St. Paul's Ecclesiological Society* (vol. 9, pp. 15–24); and a little book, *The Brasses of our Homeland Churches*, published in 1923. In these Gawthorp draws interesting comparisons between ancient and modern methods of engraving. He says, 'There is little doubt that the earliest brass engraving was conducted in exactly the same manner as in the present day, and with tools the points of which were like those of today' (*Notes and Queries*, 11 March 1922).

He amplifies this comment in his little book, where he says,

> When some brasses at Ludon (Beds.) were removed from the floor several clues to the kind of tools with which these brasses were engraved were brought to light. The Ackworth Brass (1513) was relaid in its matrix and attached to the wall. In the marginal lettering, at the top right-hand corner is the word 'TIMOR' and in the letter 'I' there is a narrow strip of brass in the centre of the down stroke. This means that the engraver with an angular graver cut an outline on each side of the stroke of his letters leaving a strip of metal between, which he afterwards cut away with a flat chisel. In this particular letter he omitted the latter process and we have in it a proof that he cut his lettering exactly as we do at the present day.

An illustration in the book shows an engraver, who had spent over fifty years in the same workshop, working on one of the figures for the Sledmere War Memorial (plate 72). This is a memorial to Colonel Sir Mark Sykes, officers and men of the West Yorkshire Regiment. The figures fill the panels of the village cross at Sledmere in Yorkshire, dressed in the style of the fourteenth century.

The same men who engraved these panels had also repaired ancient brasses, and re-engraved lost fragments. In fact there had been a considerable amount of restoration work on brasses during the latter half of the nineteenth century, stimulated by the renewed interest in medieval art and the restoration of churches which was the result of the Gothic Revival. The work varies greatly both in quality and accuracy. Some restorations are purely conjectural (e.g. Bishop Ralph Walpole, d. 1301, engr. c. 1755: plate 1). Some are based on surviving records, and some complete missing portions of mutilated brasses. The brass to Edmund Tudor, Earl of Richmond, d. 1456, engr. c. 1872–5 (plate 73) is an example of a conjectural restoration, carefully and handsomely done by the Waller Brothers. On the other hand the brasses to Sir Roger Bellingham and his wife, d. 1544, are crudely designed figures made by a local engraver, William Garside, in 1863, who shaped the plates so oddly in order to fit the indents (plate 74). Somewhat more attractive are the conjectural restorations at Maids Moreton, Bucks. (plate 75) and Worcester Cathedral (plate 76), although they would never fool the experienced eye. At least such brasses are a better form of memorial than an empty slab.

The Waller brothers were responsible for much careful restoration carrying out a lot of work on the fine series of medieval brasses at Cobham and Lingfield in Surrey. Gawthorps also restored lost brasses, as at St Alban's Abbey, Herts. (Robert Fairfax and wife, d. 1521, restored 1921) and advised on the care of modern brasses.

In *Notes and Queries* for 1 June 1929 W. E. Gawthorp suggests three precautions to prevent corrosion:

1 Use good metal. Copper predominates in fourteen-century brasses, zinc and lead in sixteenth-century ones.
2 A good varnish well backed (lacquer has no lasting qualities).
3 Use of an oak or teak mounting board: occasional application of paraffin or wax polish.

Gawthorps maintained the high traditions of craftmanship which had characterised the best of the nineteenth-century designers and engravers, until the business was taken over in 1936 by Wippells.

By the 1930s, however, very few figure brasses were being laid down. They were not only less fashionable but also increasingly expensive as a form of memorial. The brasses to Lieutenant-Colonel F. T. H.-Bernard at Nether Winchendon (plate 79), the Kendall brass at Hatfield Hyde (plate 78) and the Trollope brass in Seoul Cathedral, Korea (plate 77) are fine examples of engraving, but no longer represent the output of large metalworking firms. Instead they are the products of individual artist-engravers, as are those by the Rev. Allan Gairdner Wyon in the early 1940s (plate 80). Even today figure brasses are still occasionally engraved, and the most recent example is the interesting memorial to the late Duke of Norfolk which was unveiled in 1979 in the Fitzalan Chapel of Arundel Castle, Sussex (plate 82). Unfortunately the contemporary distaste for elaborate commemoration makes it unlikely that there will be many other such memorials.

Plate 61

THE REV. DR RICHARD TEMPLE WEST, d. 1893, St Mary Magdalene, Paddington, London. He was the first vicar of the parish he had founded in 1865. He oversaw the building of the church, designed by G. E. Street. He stands under a canopy, wearing full eucharistic vestments and holding a chalice. It was probably designed by John Ninian Comper, who designed various fittings in the church, including the fine crypt chapel of St Sepulchre. Height of figure: 45

In lumine tuo videbimus lumen

JESU   MERCI

Ricardus Temple West A Ms Ædis Christi apud Oxonienses
quondam Alumnus hanc ecclesiam ædificandam ornandam diligendam
curavit eidem XVII annos primus Vicarius profuit xᵐᵒ die Febr
Aᴰ MDCCCXCIII obiit Cujus animæ propicietur Deus Amen

Plate 62

THE REV. WILLIAM SKIPSEY SANDERS, d. 1901, chancel, St Nicholas, Guildford, Surrey.
A very fine brass showing him in eucharistic vestments under a highly ornate canopy with
St Nicholas and St Catherine in the side-shafts. Sanders was rector from 1884 to 1901 and
during his time reintroduced the use of eucharistic vestments. The brass, which shows a
remarkable resemblance to Dr West's brass in St Mary Magdalene, Paddington (plate 61),
was made by Barkentin & Krall. It may be another of Comper's designs.
78 by 37

Requiem æternam dona eis Domine
et lux perpetua luceat eis

☩ In piam memoriam Gulielmi
Skipsey Sanders istius parochiæ
olim Rectoris Petam R obdormivit in
Domino Die xu mensis Aprilis Mdcccc

Plate 63

JACK SOUTHARD WATNEY, d. 1901, Birchanger, Essex. The plate describes him as:

Lieut: XI Batt: I.Y. Machine Gun Commander / who, heading a Charge, was killed and buried / at Tweefontein South Africa / 25th December (Xmas Day) 1901 aged 19. / 'Be thou faithful unto death and I will / give thee a crown of Life' – Rev ii–10. / Erected by relatives of this Parish, to whom he was near and dear.

23½ by 32½

Plate 64

LADY MARY ISABELLA DUCKWORTH, 1902, St David's, Exeter, Devon.
The emblematic figure of an angel holding the inscription on a scroll surrounded by a
marginal inscription in bold Gothic black-letter. Heraldic lozenges are set in the angel's
wings. The inscription reads:

Giving thanks to God for / mary isabella duckworth / widow of sir john thomas /
duckworth and for mary / georgiana their daughter / march and september mcmii

The brass was designed by Byam Shaw.
50 by 26

Plate 65
GEORGE RIDDING, Bishop of Southwell, d.
1904, Winchester College chapel, Hants.
A figure in rochet, chimere, lawn sleeves
with ruffs at the wrists, and a Canterbury
cap.
Above is his coat-of-arms, with mitre and
infulae. The inscription beneath reads:

S. M. Georgii Ridding S.T.P. episcopi /
primi Southwellensis qui hujusce / Collegii
intra muros natus fuit Scho / laris
Hostiarius Informator Socius / Obdormivit
in Christo die xxx° mens / Sextil: A. S.
mcmiv aetatis suae lxxvii°.

Set in a black marble slab.
67 by 21

S·M·GEORGII·RIDDING·S·T·P·EPISCOPI
PRIMI·SOVTHWELLENSIS·QVI·HVJVSCE
COLLEGII·INTRA·MVROS·NATVS·FVIT·SCHO
LARIS·HOSTIARIVS·INFORMATOR·SOCIVS·
OBDORMIVIT·IN·CHRISTO·DIE·XXX°·MENS·
SEXTIL:A·S·MCMIV·AETATIS·SVAE·LXXVII°·

Plate 66

THE REV. RICHARD HENRY WHITE, d. 1905, Little Bardfield, Essex.
A miniature brass showing the rector standing in eucharistic vestments under a canopy
with vine leaves interwoven about the shafts. There is a scripture quotation underneath:
'Lord I have loved the habitation of Thy House and the place where thine Honour
dwelleth.'
17 by 10

Plate 67

THE REV. CANON VERNON MUSGRAVE, d. 1906, St Peter's, Hascombe, Surrey.

Musgrave was rector of Hascombe from 1862 to 1906, and it is to him that the present church owes its existence. The old church was in decay when he became rector. In his words, the churchyard was 'dark and gloomy, abounding in tall weeds and rank grass, with high mounds of graves piled up and carelessly kept'. Musgrave decided that rebuilding was the only solution and so Henry Woodyer, a pupil of William Butterfield, was appointed architect. The new church, built at a cost of £3,100 was consecrated in 1864. It is in thirteenth-century style, of Bargate stone, with a shingled bellcote, and consists of nave, chancel and Lady Chapel.

Musgrave's brass lies on the chancel floor, before the altar rails, and shows him wearing a long gown with very large sleeves, and a scapula over his shoulders. His face is adorned with a splendid beard. Around the figure is a fillet inscription, bearing these words:

In Memory of The Reverend Vernon Musgrave Master of Arts and Canon of the Cathedral Church of Winchester / who having fulfilled the duty of Rector / of this Parish for over 44 years gave up his soul to God on the 8th day of October A.D. 1906 on whose / soul may Jesu have mercy Amen.

There are shields at the four corners of the slab.
Height of figure: 53

who having fulfilled the duty of Rector of this Parish & for over 22 years gave up his soul to God on the 8th day of October A.D. 1800 on whose soul Jesu have mercy. Amen. In Memory of The Reverend Vernon Musgrave Master of Arts and Canon of the Cathedral Church of Chichester

Plate 68

THE REV. THOMAS CARLETON SKARRATT, d. 1908, Kemsing, Kent.

Skarratt stands, in eucharistic vestments, and holding the chalice and host, under a double canopy. A scroll issues from his mouth on which is 'Jesu mercy'. His shield of arms hangs from the central pillar of the canopy, a chevron between two animals (squirrels?). The whole composition is very pleasing, and well engraved. The face is obviously intended to be a portrait. The inscription reads:

Thomas Carleton Skarratt vicar of Kemsing from / A°D^{ni} 1889 who died 3 Sep^t 1908 and is buried in / the churchyard. During his vicariate the North Aisle / was built and the church and Screen restored. He adorned / the Chancel Lord I have loved the habitation of / thy house and the place where thine honour dwelleth.

Height of figure: 33

Thomas Carleton Skarratt vicar of Kemsing from
Aᵒ Dⁿⁱ 1889 who died 3 Sepᵗ 1908 and is buried in
the churchyard. During his vicariate the North Aisle
was built and the church and Screen restored. He adorned
the Chancel ✠ Lord I have loved the habitation of
thy house and the place where thine honour dwelleth

Plate 69

THE REV. NEWTON MANT, MA, d. 1911, Hendon, Middlesex, on the north wall of the church. A nicely engraved figure brass set in a round-headed recess in a stone with mouldings, the incisions filled with pigment. The vicar is shown kneeling at a desk in clerical robes, and underneath is a rectangular plate, on which is engraved in black letters the following inscription:

To the glory of God and in affectionate remembrance of / Newton Mant MA vicar of this Parish from mdccclxxxxii / to mdccccvii He was afterwards Rector of Cossington / Leicestershire where he died and was buried in may / mdccccxi His many friends in Hendon have placed this / memorial in this Church which he did much to beautify / in grateful recollection of his xv years faithful and devoted / ministry a Man well beloved.

The figure is an almost exact copy of part of the brass to Geoffrey Fyche, 1537, St Patrick's Cathedral, Dublin (see plate 70).
Inscription: 8½ by 18

Plate 70

GEOFFREY FYCHE, 1537, St Patrick's Cathedral, Dublin.

Fyche's brass shows the interior of a room, the walls lined with linen-fold panelling, and with Fyche kneeling before an altar above which is placed a Pietà. This shows Our Lady of Pity supporting the dead body of Christ (see also the brass to Thomas Elyngbrigge, 1497, Carshalton, Surrey). She is surrounded by disciples and helpers including St Mary Magdalene, the whole scene appearing as a retable or picture at the back of the altar. During the fifteenth and sixteenth centuries there was an increase in the number of these representations on brasses. Compositions including kneeling figures required a central feature to explain the devotional attitude of those commemorated. This is a good example of the genre.

Height: 25

127

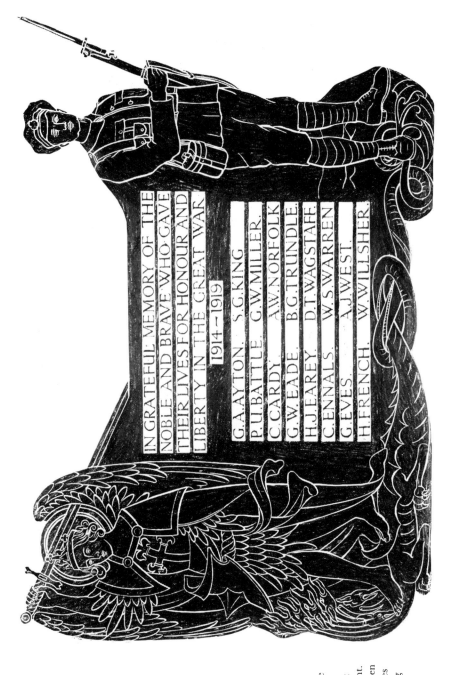

IN GRATEFUL MEMORY OF THE
NOBLE AND BRAVE WHO GAVE
THEIR LIVES FOR HONOUR AND
LIBERTY IN THE GREAT WAR
1914—1919

G.A.AYTON.	S.G.KING
P.U.BATTLE.	G.W.MILLER.
C.CARDY.	A.W.NORFOLK
G.W.EADE.	B.G.TRUNDLE.
H.J.EAREY	D.T.WAGSTAFF.
C.ENNALS.	W.S.WARREN
G.EVES.	A.J.WEST.
H.FRENCH.	W.WILLSHER.

Plate 71
WAR MEMORIAL, 1919,
Marks Tey, Essex.
St George kills the
dragon on the left of the
inscription while a
soldier stands, bayonet
at the ready, on the right.
It commemorates sixteen
men who gave their lives
for their country during
the First World War.
24 by 33

Plate 72
An engraver who had spent over fifty years in W. E. Gawthorp's workshop cutting out one of the figures for the Sledmere War Memorial, Yorks. Notice the way he holds the graver and the other tools lying on the bench.

Plate 73
EDMUND TUDOR, Earl of Richmond, d. 1456. St David's Cathedral, Pembs.
Edmund Tudor was father of Henry VII, and his tomb originally stood in the Greyfriars, Carmarthen. At the Dissolution of the Monasteries the tomb was transferred to St David's (c. 1540) by order of King Henry VIII. During the Civil War it was despoiled by Parliamentary troops. It was restored c. 1872–5 at the expense of the Rev. John Lucy, the restoration being carried out by Messrs Waller of Bolsover Street, London, at a cost of £178. The brass, which is a reasonably faithful representation of the original, is placed on a table tomb of Purbeck marble, which lies in the chancel before the high altar.
51 by 27

Heu Regum Genitor, et Frater splendidus heros,
Animis quo micuit Regia Virtus, obiit.
herculeus Comes ille tuus Richmondia Duxque
Conditur Edmundus his quoque Marmoribus,
Qui Regni Clypeus, Comitum Flos, Malleus hostis,
Vite Dexteritas, Pacis Amator erat.

hic meditare mans, te semper vivere posse,
Non morieris homo, nonne miselle vides,
Telar quem tremeret Armis, nec vinceret hector
Ipsa debitum Morte ruisse virum.
Cede metrum precibus, det Regum Conditor almus,
Eius spiritus, lucida Regna, poli.

Plate 74
SIR ROGER BELLINGHAM, d. 1544, and wife, Kendal, Westmorland.

The original brasses have long been lost. These figures were made by a local engraver, William Garside, in 1863, as replacements. The armour and dress are very freely rendered, and the figures are engraved on oddly shaped plates of metal to fit the indents.

Height of figures: 36½

THE PEOVER sisters, c. 1450, engraved in 1890, Maids Moreton, Bucks.
Two ladies wearing flowing cloaks tied with long tassels, with long flowing hair and chaplets of flowers on their heads. A lap-dog sits at the foot of each. There is an inscription beneath which reads:

In pious memory of two Maids daughters of Thomas Pever patron of this benefice / these figures are placed in the ancient matrix by M. T. Andrewes Lady of the / Manor in 1890 Tradition tells that they built this church and died about 1480.

Although the two shields are original, the figures are improbable reconstructions.

In pious memory of two Maids daughters of Thomas Pever patron of this benefice.
These figures are placed in the ancient matrix by H. H. Andrewes Lady of the
Manor in 1890. Tradition tells that they built this church and died about 1480

Plate 76

SIR GRIFFITH RYCE and wife, d. 1522, engraved c. 1860, Worcester Cathedral.
A man and woman in what the engraver imagined to be sixteenth-century armour and costume. Beneath are groups of four boys and seven girls. The figures would hardly pass as originals. They were engraved by Hardmans of Birmingham.

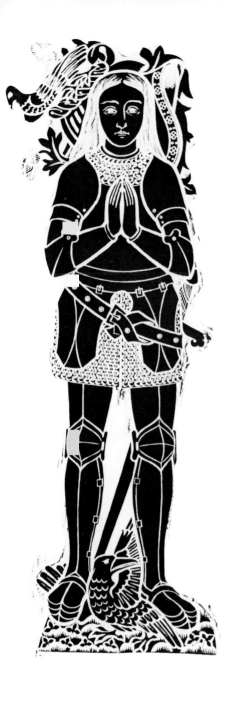

Plate 77

MARK NAPIER TROLLOPE, Bishop of Korea, d. 1930, Seoul Cathedral, Korea.
The brass is nearly life-size, showing the bishop wearing full pontifical vestments, the apparels of which are decorated with leaves, birds and fruit. His head is pillowed on a cushion decorated with his initials and the shield of the See of Korea, and he holds in his hand a model of the famous cathedral he founded. Surrounding the figure is a band divided by eight square panels. Those at the corners are the signs of the four Evangelists. In the other panels the Virgin is symbolised by a lily and St Nicholas by three balls on a book – the cathedral being dedicated to these saints. Above each is the shield of the See of Korea. The inscription reads:

Hic requiescit corpus Marci Napier Trollope, S.T.P., episcopi istius ecclesiae fundatoris / qui morte subitanea avocatus in / Domino obdormivit die 6° mens: Nov: Anno Domini 1930°, Aetatis suae 69°, & consecrationis / 20°. Cuius animae propitietur Deus.

It was designed and engraved by Mr Francis Cooper, an artist craftsman whose works cover stone carving, silversmithing, jewellery, brasses and lettering. Cooper spent 985 hours to complete the commission, which included making preliminary sketches, engraving a small self-portrait to give himself practice, and endless trouble over the details of Bishop Trollope's face. The memorial cost £200 and £58 for the stone. The plates were set into the marble slab by Messrs Hart Brothers, a firm of stone-masons in Hammersmith. The completed memorial, weighing over six tons, was then boxed up and shipped out to Korea. It is a splendid memorial and represents almost the final flowering of the art of brass engraving.

QVI MORTE SVBITANEA AVOCATVS IN DOMINO OBDORMIVIT DIE 6 MENS·NOV·ANNO DOMINI 1930·AETATIS SVAE 69 & CONSECRATIONIS 20·CVIVS ANIMAE PROPITIETVR DEVS HIC REQVIESCIT COPPVS MARCI NAPIEP TROLLOPE S T P EPISCOPI ISTIVS ECCLESIAE FVNDATORIS

Plate 78

HENRY JOHN BROUGHTON KENDALL (1840–1914), his wife and family, St Mary Magdalene, Hatfield Hyde, Herts.

The brass shows the Kendall family of Bush Hall, Hatfield, dressed in the style of c. 1914, the man in consular uniform, and his wife in a long flowing dress: the girls wear similar dresses, the boys are in Eton College suits. They were all drawn from photographs. The family's dog, Bruce, is included too.

There is a crucifix at the top of the stone, and beneath the figures an inscription in capitals, with the Kendall arms at the dexter end. It was commissioned by the late Miss Katherine Kendall (1883–1966) from Sculptured Memorials and Headstones of London, designed by the sculptor Miss Julian P. Allan, and engraved by Robert Austin, RA, in 1933–4, eventually being dedicated in 1937.

The photograph shows the inscription with certain of the dates missing. Through the good offices of Mr Richard Busby, County Librarian at Welwyn Garden City, they were eventually completed in 1973, nearly forty years after the brass was erected, by Mr George Turner of G. T. Friend, engravers, of London.

24 by 28

REMEMBER IN GOD HENRY JOHN BROUGHTON KENDALL 1840-1914 SOMETIME BRITISH CONSUL FOR BOLIVIA, GEORGIANA ISABELLA OMMANNEY HIS WIFE 1843-1923 & THEIR CHILDREN HENRY GEORGE OMMANNEY KENDALL 1866-1928 FOR 2 YEARS CURATE OF THIS CHURCH HELEN 1867 – BEATRICE 1868-1933 NEVIL 1871 – MONTAGU CHARLES 1874 – GUY 1876 – KATHARINE 1883 – WHO WORSHIPPED IN THIS CHURCH AND HELPED TO BEAUTIFY IT

Plate 79

LIEUTENANT-COLONEL FRANCIS TYRINGHAM HIGGINS-BERNARD, d. 1935, Nether Winchendon, Bucks.

Colonel Bernard is shown wearing officer's uniform of the First World War, standing on a mound of what look like Flanders poppies and resplendent in puttees. The figure is surrounded by a marginal inscription, with Evangelistic symbols at the four corners. He is described as Lord of the Manor, Sheriff of Bucks., and Master of the Skinners' Company. A quaint inscription beneath his feet sums up his virtues and achievements:

> Unto games he gave his youth
> His manhood all to rights & truth
> His age to England and to friends
> In honour here his journey ends.

This brass lies on a tomb chest against the north wall of the chancel. The tomb chest bears the family coat-of-arms and the motto: 'Bear and Forbear'. The memorial was designed by Mr Lloyd Haberly, an artist and engraver, and engraved by George Friend, engravers, 9 Dyers Buildings, Holborn, London. Extraordinarily the firm made an exact copy of this brass which was never used, and which is now in the possession of the Victoria and Albert Museum. Nothing is known about Haberly, except that he also made engravings and woodcuts for book illustrations.

Slab: 39½ by 20

LT·COL·FRANCIS TYRINGHAM

HIGGINS~BERNARD:I.P.BARRISTER AT LAW: LORD OF THIS MANOR: SOLDIER

BORN MDCCCLXIV.DIED MCMXXXV

BUCKS: MASTER OF THE SKINNERS COMPANY

SHERIFF OF IN FLANDERS

UNTO GAMES HE GAVE HIS YOUTH
HIS MANHOOD ALL TO RIGHT & TRUTH
HIS AGE TO ENGLAND AND TO FRIENDS
IN HONOUR HERE HIS JOURNEY ENDS

Plate 80

TIMOTHY REES, Bishop of Llandaff, d. 1939, Llandaff Cathedral, Glam.

The brass was originally set in a stone slab in the floor of the Lady Chapel and is now in the sanctuary there to avoid being damaged. The bishop is portrayed in full eucharistic vestments, with his mitre, and carrying a crozier in the crook of which is the lamb and cross, symbol of the Community of the Resurrection at Mirfield, of which he was a member. On the left is the shield of arms of the See of Llandaff: sable, two pastoral staves in saltire (or and argent): on a chief (azure) three mitres (or).

Rees was a legend in his own lifetime, becoming a Mirfield Father in 1907, and conducting many missions, retreats and preaching engagements throughout the country. In 1931 he became Bishop of Llandaff, at a time of great anxiety and depression in South Wales, because of large-scale unemployment. Bishop Rees made it his business to see the situation for himself – and he soon became a public figure of stature and authority. He died after over a year's illness, on 29 April 1939, and the brass was laid down subsequently. It is a fine memorial to the bishop and includes a nice human touch, showing him wearing spectacles. The inscription can be translated as follows:

In pious memory of Timothy Rees, M.C., B.A., Bishop of Llandaff 1931–9. May he rest in peace. Behold a great priest.

It is signed 'A.G. Wyon Des.' The Rev. Allan Gairdner Wyon (1882–1962), Vicar of Newlyn, Cornwall, came from a long line of engravers and medallists, his father and grandfather both having been Chief Engraver of Royal Seals. Wyon also trained as an artist and sculptor, and his chief exhibited works cover a wide range of form and materials. He designed the seals for the Archbishops of Canterbury and York, and memorials in Hereford and Salisbury Cathedrals as well as a number of memorial brasses, including that to Bishop Walter Howard Frere (d. 1938) in Truro Cathedral.

60 by 32

Plate 81

GEOFFREY HARE CLAYTON, Archbishop of Cape Town, d. 1957, Chesterfield, Derbys., south chapel of Lady Chapel.

The brass shows the archbishop standing in cope and mitre, his hands joined in prayer. His left arm holds the primatial cross to his body, and in the top left-hand corner is the coat-of-arms of Cape Town. Round the brass is a broad fillet on which are engraved the words:

Pray for the soul of Geoffrey Hare Clayton Vicar of this Parish / 1924–34 and latterly Archdeacon / of Chesterfield. Bishop of Johannesburg 1934–48 Archbishop of / Capetown 1948–57. Jesu mercy.

Clayton was Vicar and then Archdeacon of Chesterfield before going to South Africa where he was to spend the rest of his distinguished ministry. He expressed a wish in his will that no memorial be erected to him, but, in spite of that, this brass and a flagstone in St George's Cathedral, Cape Town, were laid down.

PRAY FOR THE SOUL OF GEOFFREY HARE CLAYTON VICAR OF THIS PARISH 1924-34 AND LATTERLY ARCHDEACON OF CHESTERFIELD · BISHOP OF JOHANNESBURG 1934-48 ARCHBISHOP OF CAPETOWN 1948-57 · JESU MERCY

Plate 82

BERNARD MARMADUKE, Duke of Norfolk, KG, EM, d. 1975, Fitzalan Chapel, Arundel Castle, Sussex.

The duke is shown bareheaded, in his Coronation robes, and wearing the collar of the Order of the Garter. He holds his staff of office, a sword peeps out from beneath the folds of his cloak, and around his left leg is the Garter. Below him is a short foot inscription in capital letters, giving dates of birth and death, and above are his achievement of arms and heraldic devices. The blazon of arms includes the Howard cross-crosslets fitchée, the three lions passant guardant for Brotherton, the Warren gold and blue checkers, and the Fitzalan lion rampant. Behind the shield appear the two gold batons in saltire, insignia of the Earl Marshal. Two of the duke's crests, a pair of wings issuing from a ducal coronet, and a horse holding a slip of oak foliage in its mouth, are placed on either side of the duke's figure. The third crest, a lion standing on a chapeau, sits on the helm which completes the achievement of arms.

On either side of the figure are the ribbon-like scrolls giving the duke's full title: 'Baron FitzAlan, Clun Oswaldestre and Maltravers, Baron Herries of Terregles'; 'Earl of Arundel Surrey and Norfolk'. These scrolls are in stainless steel, and, as well as being decorative, make an exciting contrast to the gold colour of the brass and the dark blue-black stone. As a wholly new idea in brass design, they have succeeded splendidly. At the top and bottom of the slab are clusters of oak leaves, and at the base, emblems of a duke, are two strawberry leaves.

The brass is set in a dark Belgian fossil-marble which has been split so that the white chapel wall shows through, thus strengthening the whole design. It was designed by Mr Christopher Ironside, who has taught at the Royal College of Art, and whose work includes some of the heraldry and decorations for the Coronation in 1953, and the reverses of our decimal coinage. The brass, which was produced at Bradford's Studios of London, weighs three and a half hundredweight. It was unveiled on 31 January 1979.

87 by 38

SOLA · VIRTUS · INVICTA

Baron · Fitz-Alan-Clune

Conditherie · Tun · Maltravers · Baron · Howard of Glossop

Surrey and Norfolk · Earl of Arundel

BERNARD MARMADUKE
DUKE OF NORFOLK · KG · EM
b · MAY 30ᵗʰ 1908 : d · JAN 31ˢᵗ 1975

Appendix A

An alphabetical
list of
known engravers

This is a list of all engravers noted so far, with dates of the period within which they operated. The most important firms are starred.

ABBOT & CO., LANCASTER St Mary, Lancaster (1916)

P. F. ALEXANDER Hepworth, Suffolk (1914); Trinity College, Cambridge (1924)

A. E. ANDERSON, UNITY STREET, BRISTOL Christ Church, Bristol (1905); Thornbury, Glos. (1918)

A. ANGEL, EXETER Combe Martin, Devon (1860)

*J. WYKEHAM ARCHER Gonville and Caius College, Cambridge (1839); Landwade, Cambs. (1846)

*A. & N. AUX, LONDON Pampisford, Cambs. (1886); Stanstead Mountfichet, Essex (1941)

J. F. BAKER, BRISTOL St Mary Redcliffe, Bristol (1864)

*BARKENTIN & KRALL, LONDON Little Paxton, Hunts. (1820); Uttoxeter, Staffs. (1933)

BARKER, YORK St Crux, York (1809)

BARR, LONDON St George's Chapel, Windsor (1874)

F. T. BARRETT & CO., BIRMINGHAM Polesworth, Warks. (1888)

BAXENDALES, MANCHESTER Leek, Staffs. (1918)

BEECHING, CANTERBURY Wilburton, Cambs. (1915)

*BENHAM & FROUD LTD, LONDON Husbands Bosworth, Leics. (1861)

BLANCHARD, HULL Holy Trinity, Hull (1893)

BLUNT & WRAY, LONDON St George's Chapel, Windsor (1903)

C. L. BLY, LONDON St Peter, Colchester, Essex (1830)

BRAYBROOK, DORCHESTER Piddletown, Dorset (1917)

BRYCESON, LONDON Ullenhall, Warks. (c.1830)

N. BUDD, WOLVERHAMPTON Lichfield Cathedral (1884); Wolverhampton (1891)

A. M. BURROW, TAUNTON AND BARNSTAPLE Taunton, Somerset (1908); (1910);
Pilton, Devon (1910)

F. M. BURTON, KING'S LYNN Newton, Cambs. (1871)

CALLCOTT, MALPAS Malpas, Ches. (1915)

CATON & CO., 64 DUKE STREET, LONDON Wath, Yorks. (1902)

CHILCOT, 291 STRAND, LONDON Ullenhall, Warks. (c.1830)

A. C. COCKSHAW, LEICESTER Kibworth, Leics. (1924)

COLMANS & CO., NORWICH Holy Trinity, Cambridge (1883); St Peter Mancroft,
Norwich (1921)

W. I. CONNOLLY Wolverhampton (1918)

COOPER, UNION STREET, PLYMOUTH Callington, Cornwall (1898)

COWEN, LIVERPOOL Ormskirk, Lancs. (1912)

*COX & BUCKLEY Castle Camps, Cambs. (1860); Chislehurst, Kent (1911)

*COX & SONS St Botolph, Cambridge (1840); Stoke Rochford, Lincs. (1880)

J. CROFT, CHESTER Tarvin, Ches. (1883)

CULN (GAWTHORP) St George's Chapel, Windsor (1895); Portsmouth Cathedral
(1918)

DALLINGER, NORWICH Elsing, Norfolk (1843)

DANBY, SOUTH MOLTON STREET, LONDON Bowness, Westmorland (1830)

W. F. DIXON Prestbury, Lancs. (1879)

H. EAST, NORWICH Hempnall, Norfolk (1902); Sprowston, Norfolk (1907)

ELGOOD BROS, LEICS. Leicester Cathedral (1880); (1884)

ELKINGTON & CO., MANCHESTER Manchester Cathedral (1913)

CHARLES ELLIOTT, 48 GEORGE STREET, LONDON Leicester Cathedral (1891)

EMLEY, NEWCASTLE Newcastle Cathedral (1906)

ENGRAVING CO. LTD, WOLVERHAMPTON Chesterfield, Derbys. (1914)

W. H. FEWING & SONS, TIVERTON Sampford Peverell, Devon (1912)

FLEMING, MANCHESTER Kendal, Westmorland (1888)

G. A. FLINT, 122 DRURY LANE, LONDON Thatcham, Berks. (n.d. but nineteenth century)

FORSYTH, LONDON Malvern Priory, Worcs. (1900)

J. FREEBURY, STROUD Painswick, Glos. (1848)

G. T. FRIEND, HOLBORN, LONDON Nether Winchendon, Bucks. (1935)

*T. GAFFIN, REGENT STREET, LONDON Horseheath, Cambs. (1881); St Mary the Virgin, Oxford (1904)

W. C. GARSIDE, KENDAL Kendal, Westmorland (1863)

*GAWTHORP (MATTHEWS), LONDON Penkridge, Staffs. (1897)

*GAWTHORP & SONS Barningham, Suffolk (1853); St John's College, Cambridge (1932)

C. GIBBS, STAINED GLASSWORKS, 148 MARYLEBONE ROAD, LONDON Sandy, Beds. (1860)

GILKES & SONS, READING St Lawrence, Reading (1890); (1895)

E. G. GILLECK Hatfield, Herts. (1918)

GITTINGS, WREXHAM Wrexham (1903)

T. GOODMAN & SONS, BIRMINGHAM St George's Chapel, Windsor (1922)

GOWER, LIVERPOOL Rufford, Lancs. (1918)

HACKETT, LEICESTER Lutterworth, Leics. (1907)

HADLOW, BRIGHTON Prestbury, Ches. (1915)

W. HALL, NORWICH St Peter Mancroft, Norwich (1892)

J. HALLAM, SON & CARTWRIGHT, LEICESTER Great Bowden, Leics. (1901)

HAMMERS, LONDON Warborough, Oxon. (1846)

GILES HAMPTON Duntisborne House, Som. (1819)

HANCOCK, SHEFFIELD Holy Trinity, Hull (1894)

*J. HARDMAN & CO. Chester Cathedral (1843); Bentley, Hants. (1910)

*HART & SON Coggeshall, Essex (1832); Trinity College, Cambridge (1904)

*HART, SON, PEARD & CO. Colne, Essex (1864); Farnham, Surrey (1921)

HAYES & FINCH Manchester Cathedral (1909)

*HEATON, BUTLER & BAYNE, LONDON Hereford Cathedral (1878); Snettisham, Norfolk (1918)

C. HENSHAW, EDINBURGH St Andrew the Great, Cambridge (1840); Madingley, Cambs. (1918)

HOLLAND & HOLT Arrow, Warks. (1860)

HOLLAND & SON Arrow, Warks. (1872)

HOULGATE, YORK Fakenham, Norfolk (1803)

F. B. JESPER & SON, ENGRAVERS, HARROGATE Holy Trinity, Hull (1868)

ABRAHAM JOHNSON, 20 SILVER STREET, HULL Holy Trinity, Hull (1882)

R. JOHNSON & SONS, HULL Brantingham, Yorks. (1918)

*JONES & WILLIS Geddington, Northants. (1881); Chesterton, Cambs. (1952)

DAVID K. Chesterton, Cambs. (1952)

G. K. Hitchin, Herts. (1916)

F. KEELING TEALE & CO., LONDON Trumpington, Cambs. (1896)

KEITH & CO. Bowness, Westmorland (1869); St George's Chapel, Windsor (1917)

W. B. R. LANDINI Chiddingstone, Kent (1914)

A. P. LISLE, TAUNTON South Molton, Devon (1891), linked with the Gawthorp workshop; Taunton, Som. (1900)

A. W. LOWE Methwold, Norfolk (1898)

*G. MAILE & SON, 367 EUSTON ROAD, LONDON Fingringhoe, Essex (1895); also signed as Maile Ltd; Great Bowden, Leics. (1933)

MAILES & STRANG Manchester Cathedral (1890)

MANNING & SON, TAUNTON Taunton, Som. (1910)

ALFRED MANTLE, WREXHAM Wrexham (1914)

P. T. MARKHAM, GREAT YARMOUTH Great Yarmouth (nineteenth century)

EDWARD MATTHEW, NEWCASTLE UPON TYNE Durham Cathedral (1908)

*E. MATTHEWS, 377 OXFORD STREET, LONDON St George's Chapel, Windsor (1852); Coleshill, Warks. (1859)

MATTHEWS & HODGSON, 113 REGENT STREET, LONDON Thornham, Norfolk (1883)

MATTHEWS & SONS, 135 OXFORD STREET, LONDON Lutterworth, Leics. (1881)

*MAYER & CO., LONDON AND MUNICH Downham Market, Norfolk (1857); Histon, Cambs. (1899)

F. W. MILLS, MARKET PASSAGE, CAMBRIDGE Swaffham Priory, Cambs. (1887); (1902)

A. L. MOORE & CO. Witchford, Cambs. (1900); Sandy, Beds. (1914)

J. MORGAN & SONS, LONDON Doddington, Cambs. (1895)

T. MORING, LONDON Sampford Peverell, Devon (1805); (1865)

W. MORRIS & CO. (WESTMINSTER) LTD Fingrinhoe, Essex (1919)

MORRIS-SINGER, WESTMINSTER Piddlehinton, Dorset (1933)

MORRISH, WISBECH Wisbech St Mary, Cambs. (1841)

*A. R. MOWBRAY & CO. LTD, LONDON AND OXFORD Chinnor, Oxon. (1916, 1917); Abingdon, Berks. (1874)

NASH & HULL, 87 NEW OXFORD STREET, LONDON Sampford Peverell, Devon (1909)

F. NEWBY, CARDIFF Chesterton, Cambs. (1897)

*NORBURY, LIVERPOOL Malpas, Ches. (1887)

F. J. OFFORD & SONS, KING'S LYNN Methwold, Norfolk (1919)

W. OFFORD, KING'S LYNN St Margaret, King's Lynn (1888)

H. OSBORN & SONS, LEEDS St Peter, Leeds (1925)

C H. OSBORNE, WINTON Winchester College, Hants. (1868)

*F. OSBORNE & CO. LTD, LONDON Middlewich, Ches. (1910); Bishop's Sutton, Hants. (1951)

PAXTON, WILSON St Mary the Great, Cambridge (1895)

W. PEARCE LTD, BIRMINGHAM St Andrew Auckland, Durham (1884)

J. R. PEARSON, BIRMINGHAM Gaywood, Norfolk (1933)

S. PERKINS, ST AUBYN STREET, DEVONPORT Brentnor, Devon (1912)

H. PICKERING, LINCOLN Norton Disney, Lincs. (1898)

C. J. PIRCH (WALSALL) Walsall, Staffs. (1908)

PONTING BROS Landwade, Cambs. (1916)

T. POTTER & SONS, 44 SOUTH MOLTON STREET, LONDON Burton-in-Kendal, Westmorland (1888); Hereford Cathedral (1897)

*T. PRATT & SONS, LONDON Byfleet, Surrey (1887); Hargrave, Northants. (1917)

G. PRIDIE St George's Chapel, Windsor (1851)

S. RAMPLING, CAMBRIDGE Withersfield, Suffolk (1916)

RAMSDEN & CARR, LONDON Edenbridge, Kent (1912)

H. ROSE, SOUTHAMPTON St George's Chapel, Windsor (1875)

S & H Kendal, Westmorland (1976); St Mary, Lancaster (1908)

H. E. SCOTT, PLYMOUTH Bridestow, Devon (1918)

SCULPTURED MEMORIALS AND HEADSTONES, LONDON Denchworth, Berks. (1932)

SEARLE & SONS, PLYMOUTH St Mellion, Cornwall (1894)

I. SENIOR, WREXHAM Wrexham (1869)

SHRIGLEY & HUNT, LANCASTER AND LONDON Higham Ferrers, Northants. (1877);
Cartmel, Lancs. (1892)

SIBTHORPE, DUBLIN Bodmin, Cornwall (1822)

*SINGERS, FROME Datchworth, Herts. (1877); Buxford, Cambs. (1918)

*F. A. SKIDMORE, MERIDEN Holy Trinity, Coventry (1836); St George's Chapel,
Windsor (1859)

CHARLES SMITH & SONS, BIRMINGHAM AND LIVERPOOL Ormskirk, Lancs. (1878)

FRANK SMITH & CO., 15 SOUTHAMPTON STREET, LONDON Cardiff (1883); Welford,
Northants. (1885); Graveley, Cambs. (1895)

JOHN SMITH March, Cambs. (1828)

HARRY SOANE LTD, LONDON Thorney, Cambs. (1882; 1892)

SOUTHWOOD & CO., BRISTOL AND EXETER South Molton, Devon (1906)

PERCY SPRANKLING, TAUNTON Taunton, Som. (1914)

STILWELL & SONS Stoneham Aspall, Suffolk (1919)

STRATTON Newent, Glos. (1805; 1810)

SULLIVAN & SWEETNAM, SLATER STREET, LIVERPOOL Childwall, Lancs. (1867)

SWINDELLS, MACCLESFIELD Prestbury, Ches. (1831)

*T. THOMASON & CO., BIRMINGHAM Uttoxeter, Staffs. (1882); St Mary, Lancaster (1897)

W. M. TONKS & SONS, BIRMINGHAM Worcester Cathedral (1887)

VAUGHAN & BROWN, LONDON Froyle, Hants. (1881)

VAUGHAN & CO., LONDON Godmanchester, Hants. (1874)

VAUGNTON, BIRMINGHAM Newark, Notts. (1892)

WALKER & COXON, NEWCASTLE UPON TYNE Newcastle Cathedral (1903)

*WALLER BROS St Leonard, Bristol (1840); Cobham, Surrey (1866)

WALTHAM & CO., WESTMINSTER Cobham, Surrey (1903)

WARD & HUGHES, LONDON Bowness, Westmorland (1902)

WARRINGTON & CO., FITZROY SQUARE, LONDON St Mary, Lancaster (1888); Lutterworth, Leics. (1889)

WELLENS & JONES, WILMSLOW, CHESHIRE St Peter, Thetford, Norfolk (1818)

*WEYER & CO., NORWICH St Peter Mancroft, Norwich (1900)

WILLIAMS, CASTLE ARCADE, CARDIFF St John, Cardiff (nineteenth century)

H. P. WILLIAMS & CO., BARNSTAPLE Braunton, Devon (1909)

G. WILLSON, 87 GREAT CHARLES STREET, BIRMINGHAM, Walsall, Staffs. (1892)

WINTON Alton, Hants. (1871)

*J. WIPPELL & CO., EXETER AND LONDON St Andrew the Great, Cambridge (1848); Witheridge, Devon (1925)

WITCHELL & CO., BROCKLEY Cartmel, Lancs. (1910)

GEORGE WRAGGE, SALFORD Manchester Cathedral (1815; 1821)

WYNN, CHELTENHAM Great Staughton, Hunts. (1890)

*A. G. WYON Llandaff Cathedral (1942)

J. YEATES Brimpsfield, Som. (1812)

Appendix B

A list of Victorian
and modern brasses
by counties

This is a list of selected brasses, not an exhaustive and comprehensive catalogue. It is based on, but not confined to, the list published by Herbert Haines in 1861 as Appendix A of his *Manual of Monumental Brasses*, and aims to give the reader some idea of the variety of modern brasses that exist throughout the country. Most of those listed are figure brasses, although some of the more interesting or unusual inscription plates are also included. It is hoped in due course to produce a more complete list of brasses laid down after 1800. Only the bare details are given of those that are included, and, unless otherwise stated, it can be assumed that they will be found in the Anglican parish church of the particular town. The date given is usually that of death rather than that of the laying down of the memorial, as the latter is sometimes difficult to discover. The author would be very grateful to hear of any corrections or additions to this list.

ENGLAND

Bedfordshire
Hawnes JOHN BARON CARTERET, 1849
Luton ALBERT BECKWITH, 1961

Berkshire
Blewbury ELIZA MACDONALD and son, 1841–9
Denchworth REV. H. B. HYDE, 1932
Finchampstead REV. E. ST JOHN and wife, 1851
Longworth ANTHONY FITZWILLIAM HYDE, 1944; DR. J. R. ILLINGWORTH, 1915
Maidenhead (All Saints', Boyne Hill) REV. WILLIAM GRESLEY, 1876; CANON
     ARTHUR DRUMMOND, 1925
Midgham REV. JOHN TURBUTT
Newbury (Newtown) FIRST LIEUT. W. E. COCKELL, 1866

Reading (Earley St Peter) HERBERT WILLIAM and HERBERT REITH DUNLOP, 1913
Shinfield MARY RUSSELL MITFORD, 1842
Theale MRS SOPHIA SHEPPARD, 1848
Wargrave COLONEL R. WHITE, 1844
Welford REV. WILLIAM NICHOLSON, 1878
West Shefford REV. THOMAS ASHLEY, 1851
Windsor (St George's Chapel) DUCHESS OF GLOUCESTER, 1859; ALAMAYU, PRINCE OF ABYSSINIA, 1879
Yattendon ALGERNON SIMEON, 1924

Buckinghamshire

Aylesbury FRANCES STUBBS, 1877
Burnham Abbey REV. ARNOLD PINCHARD, 1935
Eton (College chapel) REV. J. G. MOUNTAIN
Maids Moreton THE PEOVER SISTERS, engr. 1890
Marlow (RC) DAME MARGARET MORRIS, 1842
Medmenham ELIZA MURRAY, 1837
Nether Winchendon LIEUTENANT-COLONEL F. T. HIGGINS-BERNARD, 1935

Cambridgeshire

Cambridge (Gonville and Caius College) DR M. DAVY, 1839
Cambridge (Trinity College) REV. W. J. BEAMONT, 1868
Cambridge (Sidney Sussex College) ROBERT PHELPS, 1811
Cambridge (St Mark's) AUGUSTUS ARTHUR VANSITTART, 1882
Ely (Cathedral) GEORGE BASEVI, 1845; PRIOR JOHN CRAUDEN, engr. 1870; HESTER SPARKE 1829; BISHOP SPARKE and wife, 1836; BISHOP J. R. WOODFORD, 1885; BISHOP ALWYNE COMPTON, 1906
Fen Drayton REV. G. SHAW, 1845
Fowlmere ANNA MARIA BLACKBURNE, 1842
Mepal FRANCIS and MEYRICK DAUBENEY, 1871
St Neot's BRASS FRIEZE
Sawston RICHARD HUDDLESTON, 1847; SARAH HUDDLESTON, 1848; EDWARD HUDDLESTON, 1852
Stow cum Quy THOMAS and ELEANOR MARTIN, 1847

Cheshire

Chester (Cathedral) J. S. HOWSON, Dean of Chester, 1885; CANON M. D. TAYLOR, 1845
Chester (St John's) REV. W. MASSIE
Tarporley LIEUTENANT-GENERAL EGERTON

Cornwall

Penrose REV. J. ROGERS, 1856
Kenwyn J. L. KIRKNESS, 1848
Truro (Cathedral) CANON A. B. DONALDSON, 1903; BISHOP W. H. FRERE, 1938; ARCHBISHOP EDWARD WHITE BENSON, 1896; REV. ARTHUR MASON, 1928; REV. ARTHUR WORLEDGE, 1919

Cumberland
    Carlisle (Cathedral) REV. W. FLETCHER
    Irthington ROBERT BELL
    Lowther EARL OF LONSDALE, 1876
    Wetheral HENRY HOWARD

Derbyshire
    Ashbourne CONSTANCE WATTS RUSSELL, 1847
    Chesterfield HENRY FOLYAMBE and wife, engr. 1879; ARCHBISHOP GEOFFREY
        CLAYTON, 1957
    Elvaston SEYMORE STANHOPE, Earl of Harrington, 1866
    Padley Chapel (near Hathersage) PRIEST
    Tideswell JOHN FOLYAMBE, engr. c. 1875

Devon
    Barnstaple THOMAS SALMON, 1847
    Babbacombe ANNA MARIA HANBURY, 1877
    Bicton JOHN BARON ROLLE
    Cheriton Bishop BISHOP R. L. PENNELL, 1872
    Clovelly member of CARY family
    Exeter (Cathedral) BISHOP JOHN HORDER, 1893; AFGHAN MEMORIAL, 1881
    Exeter (St David's) LADY DUCKWORTH, 1902
    Exeter (St Sidwell) REV. JOHN GALTON, 1878
    Exeter (Wynards Almshouses Chapel) GEORGE C. KENNAWAY, 1867
    Exeter (Whipton, All Saints') ANNA EVERARD
    Gittersham REV. T. PUTT, 1844
    Heavitree REV. A. ATHERLEY, 1857
    Kitley EDMUND P. BASTARD and wife, 1838
    Manihead SIR ROBERT W. NEWMAN, 1848; SIR ROBERT L. NEWMAN, 1854
    Monkleigh WILLIAM TARDREW, 1853
    Shaugh Prior Members of MUNFORD family, 1761–1855
    Torquay (Pitt House Schools) SARA HORNBY, SUZANNE and MARY WALLER,
        engr. c. 1850

Dorset
    Caundle-Purse LIEUTENANT-COLONEL HUDDLESTON
    Melbury BRIGADIER-GENERAL T. FOX STRANGEWAYS, 1854
    Moreton JAMES FRAMPTON, 1844
    Sherborne (Abbey) WALSINGHAM GRESLEY, 1833; COUNTESS OF BRISTOL, 1858;
        EARL DIGBY, 1856
    Thorncombe SIR THOMAS BROOK, engr. c. 1860
    Whitchurch Canonicorum REV. J. R. W. STAFFORD, 1921

Durham
    Durham (Cathedral) BISHOP LEWIS DE BEAUMONT, engr. 1951

Essex
   Bardfield, Little REV. R. H. WHITE, 1905
   Birchanger JACK SOUTHARD WATNEY, 1901
   Layer Marney T. H. ST JOHN BOYS, 1897
   Marks Tey WAR MEMORIAL, 1919
   Ockendon, North REV. E. F. EVANS, 1933

Gloucestershire
   Bristol (St Leonard and St Nicholas) REV. JOHN EDEN, 1840
   Bristol (Cathedral) REV. J. R. PALMER-PALMER, 1885; CAPTAIN JOHN SANDERSON
   Bristol (Clifton, All Saints') REV. R. RANDALL
   Gloucester (Cathedral) REV. JOHN KEMPTHORNE; REV. H. HAINES, 1872
   Highnam THOMAS GAMBIER-PARRY, 1888; SIR HUBERT PARRY, 1918
   Upper Slaughter REV. FRANCIS EDWARD WITTS

Hampshire
   Bighton ENSIGN RICHARD DEANE
   Christ Church (Priory) SIR P. F. SHELLEY, 1889; ANNE PUGIN, 1832
   Hartley Westpall REV. J. KEALE, 1852
   Hayling Island D. P. MCEWEN, 1913
   Headbourne Worthy MRS E. MATTHEWS, 1884
   Highfield COLONEL E. J. CRABBE
   Hursley REV. JOHN KEBLE, 1866
   Laverstock JOHN PORTAL, 1848
   Portswood HARRIET CRABBE, 1848; ARTHUR BRANDON, 1847
   Ryde (Isle of Wight) LIEUTENANT KENT, RN
   Stansted MRS A. H. DIXON, 1846
   Winchester (College Chapel) GEORGE PROTHERO ROCH, 1858; WILLIAM HENRY
      GUNNER, 1859; SYDNEY LAW MALET, 1860; ROBERT MARRIOTT, 1868; MARTMUS
      WHITE BENSON, 1878; GENERAL W. L. PAKENHAM, 1887; BISHOP GEORGE
      RIDDING, 1904

Herefordshire
   Hereford (Cathedral) GEORGE TERRY, Esq.; BISHOP RICHARD MAYO, engr. 1857
   Pembridge Castle (private chapel) BISHOP HEDLEY BARTLETT and wife, c. 1925

Hertfordshire
   Anwell, Great FRIAR, engr. 1968
   Ardsley REV. W. W. MALET, 1885
   Essendon CORNET H. F. DIMSDALE; T. R. C. DIMSDALE
   Harpenden SIR JOHN BENNET-LAWES, 1900; MARY VAUGHAN, 1901
   Hatfield Hyde H. J. B. KENDALL and family, engr. 1933
   Hitchin REV. GEORGE GAINSFORD, 1911
   King's Langley JOHN GROOM, 1900
   Northchurch PETER THE WILD BOY, 1785

St Alban's (Abbey) ROBERT FAIRFAX, engr. 1921

Ware (St Edmund's College) BISHOP J. TALBOT, engr. C. 1840; REV. H.
CODDINGTON, 1845; REV. W. P. TILLBURY, 1863; JOSEPH PATRICK MCFAN, 1849;
REV. FREDERICK RYMER, 1910; REV. ROBERT BUTLER, 1902; HENRY EDWARD
O'REILLY, 1902; REV. CONSTANTINE LOW, 1850

Watford HON. R. CAPEL, 1857

Kent

Allington HON. J. W. STRATFORD and wife, 1850

Biggin Hill REV. V. SYMONS, 1976

Bromley LIEUTENANT-GENERAL SIR G. H. B. WAY, 1844

Chislehurst LIEUTENENT-COLONEL C. L. ALLEN, 1911; L. W. MCARTHUR, MC, 1917

Eltham LIEUTENANT L. N. MALCOLM, 1854

Folkestone REV. CANON WOODWARD

Hythe HAMILTON family, 1912

Kemsing REV. T. C. SKARRATT, 1908

Penshurst HENRY VISCOUNT HARDINGE, 1856

Ramsgate (St Augustine's Abbey) JOHN HARDMAN POWELL, 1897; ANNETTE
and LEWIS PENISTON, 1872 and 1869; REV. A. LUCK, 1864; DOM. W. ALCOCK,
1882

Rochester (Cathedral) CAPTAIN COOPER, 1858

Lancashire

Bolton REV. THOMAS RIMMER, 1848

Childwall C. OKILL, 1867

Garstang ENSIGN GEORGE WELD

Grimsagh (Chapel) REV. and MRS W. CROSS, 1849

Halton HERBERT DAVIES, 1900

Hornby REV. JOHN LINGARD, 1851

Liverpool (St John's, Tuebrook) PRIEST

Liverpool (St Margaret's, Prince's Road) ROBERT HORSFALL, 1881

Lancaster (RC Cathedral) COULSTON family, 1859; WHITESIDE family, 1867;
REV. RICHARD BROWN, 1868

Manchester (Cathedral) REV. EDWARD MCCLURE, 1906

Manchester (Salford St John's (RC)) DANIEL LEE, Esq.; JOHN LEAMING, Esq.

Manchester (Worsley) HON. ARTHUR F. EGERTON, 1866

Prescott GEORGE CAS, Esq. and wife, 1836

Preston JOSEPH S. ASPDEN, Esq.

Rainhill BARTHOLOMEW BROTHERTON, Esq.; HON. GILBERT STAPLETON

Rochdale (St Chad's) Brasses to DEARDEN family, 1847

Warrington THOMAS LYON, Esq., 1859

Worsley HON. GRANVILLE EGERTON, 1851

Leicestershire

Cadeby MRS L. K. U. MORRIS, 1974

Launde Abbey E. and M. DAWSON, 1845

Leicester (St Mary's) ARTHUR BRANDON, Esq.
Leicester (Cathedral) BISHOP R. WILLIAMS, 1979
Wanlip C. F. DAWSON, 1892

Lincolnshire
Boston REV. JOHN COTTON
Hacconby SAMUEL HOPKINSON, 1841
Horbling REV. T. BROWN, 1849
Lincoln (St Ann's) SUSANNAH SIBTHORP, 1826
Sleaford WILLIAM WELBY, Esq.
Witham-on-the-Hill REV. L. H. COOLEY, 1953

London
All Saints', Margaret Street DOM. BERNARD CLEMENTS
Holy Trinity, Sloane Street LOUISA GRACE CORNWALL, 1856
St Paul's Cathedral GARRISONS OF TRANSVAAL, 1881; RT HON. G. S. NOTTAGE,
    1885; SIR JOHN MILLAIS, 1896
Westminster Abbey GENERAL SIR R. WILSON, 1849; BISHOP J. H. MONK, 1856;
    JOHN HUNTER, 1859; ROBERT STEPHENSON, 1859; SIR CHARLES BARRY, 1860;
    SIR GEORGE GILBERT SCOTT, 1878; G. E. STREET, 1881; J. L. PEARSON, 1897
Chelsea (St Mary's (RC), Cadogan Street) SIR JOHN SIMEON, 1870
Greenwich (Our Lady of the Sea) REV. RICHARD NORTH, 1860
Paddington (St Mary Magdalene) DR R. T. WEST, 1893; REV. W. H. BLEADEN,
    1909
Southwark (St George's (RC) Cathedral) HON. EDWARD ROBERT PETRE, 1848
Streatham (St Leonard's) WILLIAM DYCE, 1864
St John's Wood EDWARD WALLIS, 1844

Middlesex
Hendon REV. N. MANT, 1911
Kensal Green (Cemetery) LADY FRANCES COLE, 1847
Kingsbury VICESIMUS KNOX, 1855; F. I. NICHOLL, 1893

Norfolk
Feltwell REV. W. NEWCOME, 1846
Hempnall BOER WAR MEMORIAL, 1902
Norwich (Bridewell Museum) REV. W. F. CREENY, 1897
Norwich (Cathedral) DEAN GEORGE PELLEW, engr. 1889
Walsingham, Little (Shrine of Our Lady) REV. W. PHILLIPS, 1935; REV. R. T.
    SADLER, 1929; REV. C. E. ROE, 1940

Northamptonshire
Carlton LADY PALMER
Grafton Underwood LADY GERTRUDE FITZ-PATRICK, 1841
Islip JOHN NICHOLL and wife, engr. 1911

Overton Longville REV. SAMUEL ROGERS
Preston Deanery REV. S. PARKINS, 1855
Tansor JOHN GASCOIGNE, 1913; REV. F. A. WALLIS, 1919

Northumberland
Felton (RC) MISS LAURA RIDDELL
Howick CHARLES, Earl Grey, 1845
Morpeth REV. JOHN BOLLAND
Newton S. COOK

Nottinghamshire
Cotgreave VEN. ARCHDEACON BROWNE
Elston REV. HENRY HARRISON

Oxfordshire
Dorchester (St Birinus (RC)) JOHN and ELIZABETH DAVEY, 1849; REV. E.
    NEWSHAM, 1859
Oxford (All Souls College) H. P. CHOLMONDELY, 1905; C. A. WHITMORE, 1909;
    E. LANE, 1914
Oxford (St Mary Magdalen) BAKER MORRELL
Yarnton A. FLETCHER, 1826

Rutland
Clipsham REV. MATTHEW STOW and sister, 1847
Oakham J. E. JONES, 1853

Shropshire
Shrewsbury LIEUTENANT-COLONEL WARREN

Somerset
Bath H. E. CARRINGTON
Kingsweston HENRY DICKENSON, 1842; WILLIAM DICKENSON, 1844
Knowle REV. JOHN ALLEN
Mells REV. J. BISHOP, 1823; REV. T. PAGET, 1783; REV. T. BURT, 1823
Milverton REV. T. TREVELYAN, 1848
Wells (St Cuthbert's) REV. HENRY W. BARNARD, 1855
Wells (Cathedral) REV. E. GOODENOUGH, 1845; BISHOP R. BAGOT, 1854; REV. H.
    W. BARNARD, 1855
Yeovil CAPTAIN PROWSE

Staffordshire
Alton (RC) EARL OF SHREWSBURY, 1852
Aston REV. H. STANLEY, 1857; REV. J. SNEYD, 1835
Brewood (St Mary's (RC)) REV. ROBERT RICHMOND, 1850

Elford REV. JOHN HILL, engr. c. 1850

Handsworth REV. DR MOORE

Lichfield (Cathedral) LIEUTENANT-COLONEL PETER JOHN PETIT, 1852; THOMAS
WILLIAM, Earl of Lichfield, 1854; VEN. GEORGE HODSON, 1855; JAMES JORDAN
SERGEANTSON, 1866

Sandon DUDLEY, Earl of Harrowby, 1847

Stoke upon Trent THOMAS MINTON, Esq.

Suffolk

Bury St Edmund's A. WALSHAM, 1854

Flixton ADAIR family, 1859

Pakefield REV. CANON B. P. W. STATHER HUNT, 1967

Surrey

Albury (St Peter and St Paul) Brasses to members of DRUMMOND family

Guildford (St Nicholas) REV. W. S. SANDERS, 1901

Ham ADMIRAL SIR H. PARKER, 1854; CAPTAIN H. PARKER, 1854

Hascombe REV. CANON V. MUSGRAVE, 1906; E. L. ROWCLIFFE, 1898

Holmwood J. G. NICHOLS, 1873

Windlesham REV. E. COOPER, 1807

Sussex

Arundel (Fitzalan Chapel, Arundel Castle) CARDINAL E. H. HOWARD, 1892;
BERNARD MARMADUKE, Duke of Norfolk, 1975

Bognor Regis (St Wilfred's) J. HOWELL, 1904

Catsfield WAR MEMORIAL, 1855

Chichester (Cathedral) DEAN BURGON, 1888

Lewes DR G. A. MANTELL, 1853

Warwickshire

Birmingham (St Chad's (RC) Cathedral) MARY BLASHFIELD, 1854; EDWARD
PEACH, 1839; JOSEPH CARPUE, 1849; JAMES BROWN, 1851 LAWRENCE KELLY,
1914

Birmingham (St Paul's) JAMES ELKINGTON, 1856

Birmingham (Erdington, St Thomas and St Edmund (RC)) GEORGE HAIGH,
1876

Birmingham (Selly Oak, St Mary) G. R. ELKINGTON, 1865

Birmingham (Witton, All Souls') REV. L. P. BROWN, 1921

Birmingham (Handsworth, St Mary) JOHN HARDMAN, 1867

Birmingham (Oscott, St Mary's (RC)) BISHOP J. MILNER, 1826; THOMAS
STONOR, 1865; Mortuary tree brasses

Coventry (Holy Trinity) J. J. HOOK, 1878; JACOB CALDICOTT, 1897

Coventry (St Osburg's (RC)) WILLIAM PATTERSON, 1843; Crucifixion,
FULFORD family, c. 1845

Coughton SIR THOMAS THROCKMORTON
Dunchurch ELIZABETH SANDFORD; DANIEL AUGUSTUS SANDFORD
Kenilworth (RC) LIEUTENANT G. W. TURVILLE
King's Newnham LADY A. LEIGH, engr. 1852
Leamington (RC) MRS E. BISHOP
Rugby (School chapel) MRS J. F. CARTWRIGHT
Rugby (St Mary's (RC)) CAPTAIN HIBBERT
Shernbourne SAMUEL RYLAND, Esq.

Westmorland

Kendal ROGER BELLINGHAM and wife, engr. 1863
Kirkby Stephen THOMAS MASON, 1891; REV. HENRY FIELDEN, 1910

Wiltshire

Ashton Rood MRS M. A. LONG
Bishopstoke GEORGE MARKHAM, Esq., 1846
Bowood JOHN R. SEYMOUR
Burbage REV. J. S. GALE
Calne MARKHAM HEALE, Esq.
Devizes (St John's) MARY MASKELL, 1847
Knoyle HENRY SEYMOUR, Esq.
Norton Bavant JOHN BENNETT and wife, engr. nineteenth century
Salisbury (Cathedral) LOUISA DENISON, 1841; DR FRANCIS LEAR, 1850; JOHN
    BRITTON, 1857

Worcestershire

Claines CAPTAIN SAUNDERSON
Corton JOHN MERRY
Dodderhill W. H. RICKETTS
Dudley REV. G. FOX
Hanley Swan (RC) EARL OF KENMARE, 1853; T. C. HORNYHOLD, 1859; T. C.
    GANDOLFI-HORNIHOLD, 1906
Hadzor GALTON family
Kidderminster JOSEPH LEA
Madresfield JOHN REGINALD, Earl Beauchamp
Malvern REV. F. DYSON
Ribbesford CAPTAIN F. WINNINGTON-INGRAM, 1843
Spetchley ROBERT BERKELEY, 1845
Stourbridge REV. M. CREWE
Tenbury (RC) JOHN STAINER, 1859
Worcester (Cathedral) REV. CANON ST JOHN
THOMAS BAXTER, 1872; SIR GRIFFITH RYCE, engr. c. 1860

Yorkshire

Ampleforth Abbey (RC) DOM. C. HEDLEY, 1915
Birstall CANON J. KEMP, 1895
Birstwith MRS I. GREENWOOD, 1891
Bishop Thornton (RC) CANON J. PLATT, 1862
Dent ADAM SEDGEWICK, 1913
Ecclesfield J. K. BOOTH, Esq.
Fishlake REV. GEORGE ORMSBY, 1866
Grinton REV. H. A. WILLIAMS, 1920
Harewood WILLIAM LASCELLES, 1851
Harpham MATTHEW ST QUINTIN, 1876
Harrogate (St Wilfred's (RC)) REV. W. F. SWANN, 1947
Malton ARTHUR GIBSON, 1837
Mirfield THOMAS WHEATLEY, Esq.
Ripon (Cathedral) E. B. BADCOCK, 1895
Sessay GUY CUTHBERT DAWNAY, 1889
Skipton (RC) HENRY TEMPEST, 1891; TEMPEST family
Sledmere (War Memorial) COLONEL SIR MARK SYKES
Thirsk VISCOUNT DOWNE, 1856
Thornes MRS O. JONES, 1865
Wensley ALGITHA ORDE-POWLETT, 1871
York (Minister) CRIMEA WAR MEMORIAL, 1855; WAR MEMORIAL, 1921

IRELAND

Armagh REV. R. ALLOTT
Clondrohid (Cork) LIEUTENANT-COLONEL KYLE
Dublin (St Patrick's Cathedral) ARCHBISHOP TALBOT, 1919
Killarney (Cathedral (RC)) EARL OF KENMARE, 1853; CATHERINE, wife of Earl of Kenmare, 1854; BISHOP DAVID MORIARTY, 1877; T. W. MURPHY, 1860

SCOTLAND

Beauly HON. G. S. FRASER
Cumbrae (College Chapel) W. A. ROBERTSON
Dunfermline (Abbey) ROBERT THE BRUCE
Dunkeld REV. J. SKINNER, 1841
Edinburgh (St Mary's Cathedral) BISHOP WALKER, 1841; BISHOP DOWDEN, 1910; BISHOP A. CAMPBELL, 1921; BISHOP H. S. REID, 1943
Pitlochry (River Ardle) QUEEN VICTORIA's Tea Party, 1866
Portallock N. MALCOLM
Rosslyn (Chapel) HARRIET COUNTESS ROSSLYN

WALES

Aberdovey LORD ATKINS, 1940
Abergele REV. R. JACKSON
Gresford REV. C. PARKINS, 1843
Haverfordwest BARON and BARONESS MILFORD
Llandaff (Cathedral) BISHOP T. REES, 1939
Llanilar JOHN WILLIAMS, Esq.
Llanover MRS F. L. H. BERRINGTON
Llangynfelyn JANE GILBERTSON, 1810
Northop REV. R. HOWARD, 1860
Pennal THRUSTON family, c. 1855
Ruthyn VEN. NEWCOMBE
St David's (Cathedral) EDMUND TUDOR, engr. 1875

AMERICA

Elberon, New Jersey (St James) PRESIDENT JAMES GARFIELD, 1881
Brooklyn, New York (St Anne) THOMAS MESSENGER, 1881
Halifax, Nova Scotia (St Paul) LOUISA BOLDERN, 1826

ASIA

Korea (Seoul Cathedral) BISHOP M. N. TROLLOPE, 1930

Index

Numbers in italics refer to plate numbers